CARE TO COMPETE

CARE TO COMPETE

A COACH'S GUIDE TO CONNECTION THAT WINS THE MARGINS

Hunter Price

Care to Compete
A Coach's Guide to Connection That Wins the Margins
Copyright © 2026 by Hunter Price

Disclaimer: This book has been published for the purpose of providing the reader with general information on its subject matter. The author and the publisher believe the information to be accurate and authoritative at the time of publication. The book is sold with the understanding that neither the author nor the publisher is providing professional advice, and the reader should not rely upon this book as such. Every situation is different, and professional advice (whether psychological, legal, financial, tax, or otherwise) should only be obtained from a professional licensed in your jurisdiction who has knowledge of the specific facts and circumstances.

Scripture quotations taken from The Holy Bible, New International Version®, NIV®. Copyright © 1973, 1978, 1984, 2011 by Biblica, Inc. Used with permission of Zondervan. All rights reserved worldwide. www.zondervan.com.

Cover Design: Alex Demczak Demczak
Interior Layout and Design: Alice Briggs
Editorial Team: Maggie Syrett, Jamie Smith, Ginny Glass

ISBNs:
Ebook: 979-8-89165-409-9
Paperback: 979-8-89165-410-5
Hardcover: 979-8-89165-411-2

Published by:
Streamline Books
Kansas City, MO
streamlinebookspublishing.com

To the coach who believes the most important wins happen in life

CONTENTS

FOREWORD

I've coached in packed gyms and half-empty ones. I've coached under bright lights and on cracked concrete. I coached before social media, and now coach very much within it.

Here's what I know for sure: the game has changed but what players need from coaches hasn't.

Scroll long enough and you'll find endless drills, breakdowns, highlights, and hot takes. I post plenty of that myself. But behind every clip, every viral moment, and every "secret sauce" for winning, there's a question most coaches don't stop to ask: *Do my players know I care about them, or do they think I just care about the scoreboard?*

That's why this book stopped me in my tracks.

This book won't teach you about running better sets or stealing a few extra points a game. You'll learn about earning *trust*. About building culture when no one is filming. About understanding that connection is the real competitive advantage—and always has been. I'm a basketball guy, like Hunter, but this book is a must-read for coaches of all sports to read.

Hunter understands something that every great coach eventually learns: Players don't play hard for plays; they play hard for people.

In a world where players are more informed, more vocal, and more emotionally aware than ever, yelling louder isn't leadership. Control isn't culture. And fear builds distance, not toughness.

Care builds buy-in.

Connection builds accountability.

Culture wins when talent alone won't.

You'll find stories in this book that feel familiar. Practices where things went sideways. Conversations that mattered more than any time-out. Moments where choosing care over ego changed everything. Hunter doesn't romanticize coaching—he tells the truth. And that's exactly what today's coaches need.

So if you're a coach trying to figure out how to lead the next generation of athletes . . .

If you're tired of pretending you have it all figured out . . .

If you believe sports can still shape lives, not just résumés . . .

This book is for you!

The best coaches don't go viral for how much they know; they're remembered for how they made people *feel*. Read this book. Share it with your staff. And then go coach the game the right way, one relationship at a time.

Matt Hackenberg
High School Basketball Program-Building Expert and Strategy Specialist

INTRODUCTION

Locker rooms have shaped much of my life. From the first days of youth sports through high school competition, they became classrooms for lessons in teamwork, leadership, and perseverance. After graduating high school in the spring of 2011, that passion for the game naturally evolved into a calling to coach. During college, I volunteered at camps and with local teams, learning from outstanding mentors and studying what separated good programs from great ones. Those experiences led to my first official coaching opportunity and eventually to my becoming one of the youngest varsity basketball coaches in the state of Wisconsin.

When I took over the program, it had managed more than fourteen wins only once in school history. Within three years, our team set school records for total victories, postseason wins, points scored, and playoff advancement. The turnaround didn't happen because we had the best talent, facilities, or funding. Change happened because we built a culture where players cared more about the team than themselves. When hearts align behind a shared mission, the results can exceed what anyone expects.

Every coach will face opponents with advantages—better resources, deeper rosters, or greater name recognition. What evens the playing field is chemistry. Preparation, effort, attitude, and selflessness are choices that every team controls. When those elements come together, teams can achieve far more than the sum of their parts.

This book was written for coaches who share that belief. Whether you're waiting for your breakthrough, exploring how to strengthen your team culture, or searching for ways to compete against programs with more, my hope is that the ideas and actions in these pages will help your team grow closer, care deeper, and perform at a level that surprises everyone, including you.

Throughout the chapters ahead, you'll find a blend of personal stories, practical strategies, and team-building exercises that can be applied at any level of coaching and in any sport. The book is divided into two distinct parts. Chapters 1 to 6 focus on building understanding—what it truly means to care and how that concept shapes a team's culture. Chapters 7 to 15 shift toward application, offering strategies for growth, reflection questions, and action steps to help you immediately put these ideas into practice.

At the end of the book, you'll find our Lead 101 program. This eight-day team development guide to start your season will be the boost you need to transform your culture. By the end, you'll have a clear road map for developing a team that not only wins more games but also transforms the lives of the people within it.

CHAPTER 1

WHAT DOES IT MEAN TO CARE?

ONE THING HAS bothered me about every locker room I've ever been in: everyone, from players to coaches, says they care. But that can't be true. I coached and played for twenty years, and the words and actions I witnessed demonstrated that not everyone wearing our jersey cared about the team. Yet ask anyone if they care, and almost without hesitation, they'll raise their hand.

Right now, if you gathered your team and asked, "Who here cares about this team?" most, if not all, players and coaches would raise their hand. But do they really? Deep down, they know the truth. Some players skip workouts and still say they care. Some talk back to coaches but insist they care. Some coaches don't show up to youth camps, yet claim they care. How can people be so out of touch with their true intentions? Is it a comfortable lie they tell themselves, or a simple lack of awareness?

I wrestled with this for a while. Then one day, someone casually asked me what I cared about. I said, "I care about my wife . . . and the Green Bay Packers." I laughed at how strange that sounded. And then it hit me: Are those two things equal? Absolutely not. Not even close. But I could confidently say I cared about both. I realized that the word *care* is too broad—it doesn't capture the depth or type of commitment we're referring to.

The English language has only one word to express caring: *care*. To each person, it can mean something very different. Some languages have multiple words to express nuance in a certain category. Take Hebrew, for example. It has multiple words for different types of love: *Ahava* is romantic love; *chesed* represents deep loyalty born from love; *re'ut* is companionship love; *dod* represents physical love; and *racham* reflects the love a parent feels for a child. Imagine if we had words to describe every nuance of emotion. Misunderstandings would disappear. Now think about our locker rooms. When we ask, "Who here cares?" we're using one word to cover countless types of effort, commitment, and loyalty. It's no wonder players and coaches say they care, even when their actions don't align.

To understand care, we need more precise language, a way to measure care in action, not just words. Some players on your team care "a wife's worth." It's their entire life. They think about the team's path to success constantly. They put in work to improve when necessary. Some players care "a Green Bay Packers' worth." It moves them in the moment. When the team is winning, it's fun, but it's not something they plan their life around or think about consistently. Both groups would say they care. And that's the issue. They genuinely think they do, but in reality, they're very far apart. We have to narrow it down more to know exactly where the hearts of our teams lie.

We have to ask questions like:

- How many of you care enough not to be the star?
- How many of you care if we win or lose, even when your stats don't look good?
- How many of you care enough to show up and work hard when it's not required by the coaches?

Answers to these questions require trust. Without trust, players will tell you what you want to hear, not what's true. Few will admit selfishness; that's human nature. This book focuses on creating awareness through understanding, not forcing confession. By developing a shared language of care, your team can discuss and improve the way they commit to each other and the mission.

The equation for the type of care that includes both *actions* and *words* is very simple:

CARE = SELFLESSNESS + WORK ETHIC

The equation can't stay theoretical. It has to be lived. Selflessness and work ethic only matter when they show up in daily habits, shared language, and collective expectations. For my team, those values were reinforced every time we broke the huddle. The words we chose weren't hype; they were holding us accountable.

When we broke the huddle before games, we chanted *All In*, *Family*, or *Together*. It wasn't a slogan but a standard. Every player, coach, and staff member was committing to something bigger than themselves. To *be* any of those slogans is to care in the deepest, most selfless sense: showing up early, staying late, giving when it's inconvenient, and valuing the name on the front of the jersey more than the one on the back.

Living out that kind of commitment demands honest self-awareness. A catchy motto doesn't guarantee a win. Teams fall short because they convince themselves they're embodying their motto when they're not. And that gap between who we *say we are* and who we *actually are* becomes one of the biggest obstacles to growth.

Over time, our perception of what it means to care has shifted; it has become a Mandela Effect, a phenomenon in which a group of people confidently shares the same false memory. In a team, this happens when players collectively believe something isn't true, like thinking they always work hard, communicate well, or show up on time—simply because the group repeats it enough. It's a shared illusion of effort that feels real though results say otherwise. To understand care, we must debunk the myths we've convinced ourselves are true.

MYTH 1—ALL ACTIVITY IS EQUIVALENT TO WORK ETHIC

Legendary basketball coach John Wooden's famous quote, "Don't mistake activity for achievement," debunks this myth.[1] I coached long enough to know that not every kid in the gym was getting better. During open gym shootarounds, I'd see players tossing up half-court shots or shooting granny-style free throws. The unfortunate truth is that many of those players left thinking they had improved. They assumed that simply holding a ball for an hour meant they had shown work ethic. You can picture exactly what that looks like in your own sport. As a coach, it's your job to distinguish unwavering work ethic (effort that demonstrates care) from pseudo-work, which is just an act.

MYTH 2—BEING LIKED MEANS YOU CARE

Somewhere along the line, we've all falsely believed that because someone is popular, they must be talented or hard-working. The popular kid in school, the charismatic colleague, the doted-on sibling are all naturally assumed to have earned their status from their actions. However, popularity often has little to do with effort or skill but can be a product of charm, timing, or perception. Genuine care, work ethic, and commitment are revealed through consistent actions; they have nothing to do with applause, attention, or social standing. As a coach, it's your job to look past popularity and evaluate each player by the habits they cultivate, the effort they give, and the integrity of their commitment.

MYTH 3—CARING IS SOFT

Sadly, the general population has associated caring with weakness. In many circles, those who care are made fun of. The younger generation has labeled these people "try-hards"—my all-time least favorite name-call from kids. The goal of this mindset is to make it seem unpopular to care, so that when people don't care, it doesn't feel as wrong. As adults, we don't necessarily take it that far, but as coaches, we often fall into a similar trap. We convince ourselves that tough love is the only way to show care, that vulnerability is weak, and that obedience must be earned through strictness. That's all a lie.

Authentic leadership shows care consistently, holds others accountable with empathy, and creates an environment where vulnerability is respected, not ridiculed. Caring is strength, not weakness. It's the foundation of every team that chooses to be all in.

Care involves consistent, selfless action—showing up, holding yourself and others accountable, and prioritizing the team over individual comfort or recognition. By debunking the myths of care, creating awareness, and developing a shared language, you set the foundation for a team culture where effort, commitment, and integrity are visible in every drill, practice, and game.

The Self-Determination Theory (SDT) is a popular concept in psychology that explains what leads to a person thriving in an ecosystem. SDT provides one of the clearest psychological explanations for why some athletes thrive while others check out.

When players feel heard, capable, and connected, they're more willing to buy into something bigger than themselves.

SDT says that people are at their best when three core needs are met: *autonomy*, *competence*, and *relatedness*. As a coach, you see these play out every day.

Players need a sense of autonomy—not control over the team but the feeling that their voice matters and their effort has purpose. They need competence, the belief that they're growing, improving, and capable of contributing. And they need relatedness, the connection to their teammates and coaches that makes them feel valued. When one of these needs is ignored, motivation drops and culture suffers. But when all three are nurtured, players work hard—with heart. SDT reminds us that, along with teaching skills, great coaching creates an environment where every athlete feels empowered, capable, and connected.

These three needs—autonomy, competence, and relatedness—form the foundation for everything you want your culture to become. They're the soil from which commitment grows. When players feel heard, capable, and connected, they're more willing to buy into something bigger than themselves. Your cultural standards that were once simply rules on a wall become lived values. When these three psychological needs are met, players are ready to invest. They show up and buy in.

Coaches, if you want to compete at the highest level or punch above your weight class, you have to care. You have to connect with every heart in your locker room. When players know you care, they will go the extra mile. They won't just want to succeed; they'll want to succeed for you.

One of the greatest compliments I ever received came early in my career from an assistant coach. He said, "Coach, I don't know if you realize this, but the reason these boys are playing so hard is because they don't want to let you down. They want to see you succeed." To this day, that compliment still moves me. What I didn't fully realize until he said it was this: If you truly want to compete, priority number one, before any schematic discussion or strategic plan, is that you and your team have to care, in the same way, about the same things.

CHAPTER 2

THE FOUNDATION OF LEADERSHIP

AS I APPROACHED my thirties, I realized I needed to take a serious dive into leadership. Every significant step on my coaching journey so far had been the result of high-quality guidance from mentors, fellow coaches, and highly valued subordinates. Therefore, I started attending conferences, reading books, and seeking out anyone who could teach me something new. I wish I had homed in on leadership earlier in my career, but as the cliché says, better late than never.

There's no wrong time or wrong age to invest in learning how to lead well. One of the most important lessons I've learned is to surround myself with people who are smarter than me. It sounds obvious, but it's harder than you might think. It requires humility—the willingness to admit that you don't have all the answers—and curiosity—the drive to intentionally seek out new knowledge instead of staying in the safety of what you already know. I've met coaches who openly admit they don't want to learn from anyone else. They'll stick to what they know and call it enough.

The problem with that mindset is that you'll never grow beyond what you already understand. You might survive, but you won't thrive. To reach your full potential as a leader, you need others who push you, challenge you, and expand your perspective. An old proverb says, "As iron sharpens iron, so one person sharpens another" (Prov. 27:17). Just as iron is used to refine and strengthen another piece of iron, people challenge, push, and improve one another.

A mentor doesn't usually appear like a genie, magically showing up the moment you need help. Most of the time, you have to step out of your comfort zone and seek one out. Over the years, I reached out to several well-established coaches for guidance. I also leaned heavily on the coaches who supervised me during my years as a junior varsity (JV) coach; they became anchor points as I transitioned into varsity coaching.

In my first season as a head coach, I started the holiday break without a single win. I was gutted. The thought of going home for Christmas and facing the inevitable *How's the season going?* questions made my stomach turn. The only person I wanted to talk to was my mentor, the one person who understood my pain. Coaching is hard to explain to non-coaches. People assume they get it because they watch sports, but they don't. My mentor talked me off the ledge more times than I can count that year. And when we finally pulled off a major upset to close the season—a win no one expected—he was the first to text me an "Atta boy!" Mentorship matters.

Years later, I've had young coaches contact me on social media asking for advice or mentorship. I usually accept gladly. I remember being in their shoes, desperate for guidance, hanging on to every bit of reassurance. Helping them feels like the right way to honor the people who helped me.

Never be too nervous to ask a coach for help. The worst that can happen is that they say no! More often than not, you'll find that the coaching community is a family—and in every family, someone is always willing to help. Families support one another, but healthy families also protect their values. In coaching, care goes beyond encouraging your players to stewarding their potential. Stewardship is paramount when you encounter resistance, indifference, or entitlement in your program.

Before defining what it means to care, we need to talk about the reality every coach eventually faces: Someone on your team, or even on your staff, simply doesn't care. It could be a player participating only because a parent insists, or a coach coaching only for a paycheck. Apathy can enter a locker room in many ways. When it does, the first place to look is at yourself. If toxic or disengaged individuals keep appearing on your team, your evaluation and selection processes may be flawed. Are you measuring character during tryouts? Are your interviews thorough enough? At some point, you have to own your role as the gatekeeper of your team culture.

At some point, you have to own your role as the gatekeeper of you team culture.

What happens next depends on the type of sport you coach. If you're in a no-cut program, it might feel like you're stuck, but there are still ways to protect your culture. You'll need to have uncomfortable conversations and set clear non-negotiables. Behavior contracts are always a good idea. While you might not be able to remove someone for talent alone, you *can* hold them accountable for failing to meet expectations. Always involve your administrators to make sure you're aligned, and remember, this is a culture decision. If you set a consequence, you must be ready to enforce it. Failure to follow through destroys credibility. Never issue an ultimatum you can't or won't enforce.

In cut sports, the decision-making shifts, but the principle is the same. Not all talent is good talent. Sometimes the best decision is to cut a highly skilled player. It's rarely easy. Families will question you, administrators may challenge you, and people may second-guess your judgment.

In one of my final seasons, I made the difficult decision to cut just one player from the team. It may sound harsh, especially because he attended every open gym and every workout. On the surface, it felt counterintuitive—why cut the kid who shows up? Why not keep one more player when the roster wasn't full?

But this young man consistently made racist and lewd comments at school, and his behavior outside of school raised even more concerns. He was a walking red flag. As a coach, my responsibility was to build a team that could compete on the court and a group of young men who could thrive together, push each other, and protect the culture we worked hard to create. Keeping the player, despite his effort in the gym, would have jeopardized all that.

The next day, one of my superiors—and several others—questioned my decision. I don't blame them. Cutting just one player can look harsh from the outside. Students from the school told me I was cruel. Word got around quickly that I was a mean, heartless coach. They didn't realize that I was building a culture, a framework that would last for years, not one feel-good moment.

During the conversation with my boss, I explained my concerns about the young man's behavior and the impact it would have on the team's culture. He wasn't convinced. He suggested I give the kid a chance, reminding me that he needed love and guidance.

I agreed, every kid needs love. But playing varsity basketball is a privilege, not a right. There is a line I will not cross. I laid out the potential scenarios, all the ways this could go wrong, and how his presence could damage the program and the players who were doing things the right way. After hearing my reasoning, he finally let it go, which I respect him for.

When you make tough decisions, you must be ready and willing to defend them. If you communicate clearly and show that your choices are thoughtful, intentional, and rooted in what's best for the team, your administrators are more likely to trust your judgment.

Championships are not won by talent alone; it takes culture, alignment, and trust. Fortune favors the bold, and movements are led by the brave. When you can defend your decisions, you emerge stronger, and you send a clear message: Talent does not grant permission to behave however one pleases.

The same care and intention applies to hiring coaches. Don't settle for the first decent candidate you see. When I was hired as a freshman basketball coach fresh out of college, I was the only person interviewed. I had worked the camps all summer, I was a man of character, and I worked hard. That's all the varsity coach needed to see.

Later, a colleague, who became a good friend of mine, asked, "What if Coach K had applied? They would never have known!" His point was that although I was a solid candidate, the coach didn't do his due diligence in the interview process. He should have interviewed more candidates. It's unlikely that someone like Coach K, legendary Duke basketball coach Mike Krzyzewski, would have applied, but you never know! As much as it could have felt like an insult, my friend was right. Although the varsity coach thought I would do a good job, he couldn't be sure there wasn't someone better.

I'm grateful that he did choose me, because it set the path for my career. Be deliberate and patient. Study all options. Cast a wide net even if you think you have an easy hire.

During the interviews, watch their answers and reactions; evaluate their character as closely as their skills. Lower-level coaches are not small players in your program; they teach, develop, and represent your culture. Ten times out of ten, I'd rather hire someone with high character than high knowledge. Knowledge can be taught; integrity can't.

Look for simple but essential skills and attributes in a coaching staff member. First, *patience*—are they willing to invest in a long-term process of development, or do they demand instant success? Next, a *team-first* mindset—are they supportive when players move up from their team to another level, like JV to varsity, or do they take it personally? You also need coaches with a *passion for working with kids*—people who find joy in the grind, the growth, and the daily interactions. And finally, *trust*—can you trust them with information, ideas, and conversations that need to stay within the staff? And can you trust that they'll carry out your vision and non-negotiables?

If you're a lower-level coach looking to move up, don't take rejection personally. A wise man once told me, "Being told no doesn't mean you're not ready. It simply means you're not the right fit for them." Too often we confuse not being selected for a job with not having value. But a no from one program isn't a no from every program. Look for somewhere where your strengths, style, and vision will align better. Keep applying, keep growing, and keep trusting that the right fit will find you.

Utilizing a selective process isn't a 100 percent protection against later problems. When a coach is failing in some way, the first step is to have a hard conversation. I always tried to wait until the end of the season unless it was a drastic situation, like abuse, cheating, or total negligence. Sadly, stories abound of coaches who crossed clear, obvious lines. As the head of the program, you should not tolerate those behaviors—for the sake of the rest of the team. And remember, anything you tolerate will reflect back on you. When you care about your program, major infractions cannot go unpunished.

One of the most well-known examples of tolerating abuse within a program is the infamous Penn State football scandal under legendary coach Joe Paterno. His longtime assistant, Jerry Sandusky, abused boys for years. Paterno didn't actively approve of the behavior—but he didn't address it either and turned a blind eye. The signs were there, flags had been raised, yet the man at the top claimed ignorance. This is an extreme example, but when you avoid any problem or sweep it under the rug, you become responsible for it. As the head coach, the program is yours. What you permit, whether intentionally or by neglect, you endorse.

If the infraction doesn't cross a serious line, mid-season removal should be a last resort, because replacing someone mid-year is far harder than a temporary fix. In that conversation, be honest and specific: Tell them where they're falling short, what they need to improve, and your expectations for them moving forward. One conversation isn't enough: Consistency matters. Checking in regularly shows that you care. Consistency separates hoping for success from actively chasing it.

If improvement doesn't happen, follow through. Releasing a player or coach also demonstrates care. It positions them in a place where they can thrive while also protecting the integrity of your team. You win as a leader when you ensure that everyone in your locker room, players and coaches alike, understands the mission and embraces it. From your own growth as a leader, to selecting the right people, to holding everyone accountable, the foundation for having a culture of care begins with intention, consistency, and the courage to do what's right every step of the way.

On my leadership journey, I discovered the power of developing a universal language within a team or workplace. I'm talking about creating a shared culture of values and words that everyone understands, language that transcends backgrounds and unites people around common principles. When your players and coaches share a common language around expectations and culture, it becomes easier to build trust, set standards, and hold everyone accountable. In the chapters ahead, I'll introduce terminology your team can adopt as its universal language, starting with the four levels of care: The Sloth, The Vortex, The Ally, and The Heartbeat. I established these four levels by measuring work ethic and selflessness.

CHAPTER 3

THE SLOTH

I F WE WERE drafting animals to compete in a challenge, a sloth would probably not be considered a high-value pick. On the other hand, it wouldn't hurt your team, because it wouldn't fight with the other animals or cause drama. Someone who behaves like a sloth neither helps nor harms the team. They lack the work ethic to contribute meaningfully to the skills required for success. They're safe in terms of their character, but they lower the ceiling of your team's success.

In sports, Sloths generally care about the team and maintain a positive presence—they are players who demonstrate selflessness—but they lack work ethic. They aren't defined by talent: Some Sloths are naturally talented kids but lazy, and others are athletes who don't have talent because they don't work hard. A simple way to spot the Sloths on your team is to ask each person to point out the facility's light switches. Those who can't answer have likely never been the first to show up or the last to head out.

When asked if they care, Sloths insist they do. After all, they genuinely want the team to succeed, but *wanting* success isn't the same as *working* for it. They believe that caring is defined solely by encouragement, cheering for others and being a "good teammate." What they fail to recognize is that work ethic is an essential part of care. A Sloth convinces themselves, "As long as I support my teammates, I'm doing my part." But support without effort only wins half the battle. Their lack of discipline and effort reveals the gap between intention and investment.

TRAITS

- Is apathetic to competition
- Doesn't attend unless it's mandatory
- Doesn't cause conflict within the team
- Is fine if they're not the star of the show
- Doesn't do anything "extra" in practices

CARES ABOUT

Teammates, team success, personal comfort

DOESN'T CARE ABOUT

Extra effort, voluntary workouts

EXAMPLE

We can all agree that Sloths don't bring much to the table in competition. However, you might still take them on your team.

They're pleasant, fun to be around, and won't create drama. Although they have negative qualities, a Sloth is far less dangerous to team culture than a Vortex, which we'll discuss in the next chapter. The trade-off is that their skill level is usually lower, and you probably can't count on them for production. As the saying goes, *It's better to tame a stallion than inspire a mule.* Whether it's a mule or a Sloth, you're not likely to win many battles with them by your side.

Their lack of discipline and effort reveals the gap between intention and investment.

The most successful season I had as a coach included several Sloths on my team. They were good kids who enjoyed being part of the team. They're not detrimental if paired with talent. As long as a Sloth doesn't have to play, their impact on locker room culture is minimal. But if you need them to perform, you are in trouble. If your roster includes Sloths, you'd better have a lot of talent to pair with them.

A major problem with Sloths is that they don't push the team in practice. One of my biggest issues as the coach of a school without a large pool of athletes was that there was a massive talent drop-off on the roster. The kids who were on the scout team were genuinely good kids, but due to poor work ethic, they couldn't help the starters prepare for the games. My other coaches and I had to simulate competition to challenge the starters. The days we did scout team game prep, I threw on some old basketball sneakers and a practice jersey and hopped out there. My joints suffered, but it was necessary to prepare my guys for the next game.

If Sloths remain in a role-player capacity, your team can survive with them. Their selfless nature means they're nice to have around: they root on others, aren't bitter about playing time, don't care about stats—and you rarely hear them complain.

CONVERSATIONS TO HAVE WITH A SLOTH

A Sloth desperately needs a fire lit under them. You have to challenge their apathy. Most coaches default to being challengers; few are naturally non-confrontational. So embrace your inner coach. A Sloth needs to understand that *they must improve* to help the team they care about. They must show up more and try harder.

Don't waste this opportunity to grow your team. One effective approach is to have former players return to share their experiences, emphasizing regrets and lessons learned. Almost everyone who moves on from their sport wishes they had made more of an impact, making this a relatable and motivating talking point.

Your goal is to light a fire, to move Sloths from apathetic to motivated (note: this is easier than turning a Vortex from selfish to selfless). Typical talking points include:

- "There are kids who dream of playing on this team. They regret not playing. They have limitations, disabilities, or just didn't make the team. Any of these kids would trade places with you in a second. Don't waste this opportunity."
- "One day you'll be talking to your kids about work ethic. Do you want to be a hypocrite when telling them to try harder? Or do you want to be able to share your story with pride?"
- "You never get this opportunity back. Once your senior year ends, it's done. Don't take this experience lightly, or you'll regret it for the rest of your life."

As you deliver this message, the key is to inspire without insulting. Avoid belittling, name-calling, or shaming. Think carefully about your words before you speak.

HISTORICAL HIGHLIGHT

In professional sports, the number one draft pick is expected to turn a franchise around. Many are everything the organization hoped for and more—Peyton Manning, Bryce Harper, LeBron James, and Connor McDavid. Each one became a franchise cornerstone and an all-time great in their sport. Others, like Blake Griffin, Baker Mayfield, and Justin Upton, were talented players but didn't quite become the franchise saving mega-stars their teams hoped for.

And then there are the busts. The term may seem harsh, but in sports, a *bust* is defined as a top pick who fails to meet expectations. Causes vary: overestimated ability, lack of effort, poor work ethic, or destructive social influences.

JaMarcus Russell is a notable example of a top pick falling into the Sloth category. At LSU, he was an exceptional quarterback with a cannon arm, in an imposing six foot six, 260-pound frame. In 2007, the Oakland Raiders drafted him first overall, hoping he would transform the franchise.

Almost immediately, hopes turned to fears. Russell reportedly showed up to training camp at 300 pounds, made no effort to study the playbook, and demonstrated little interest in learning the game. At one point, coaches even handed him blank tapes labeled "game film" to see if he would study them; he claimed he had watched them the next day. His lack of preparation had two consequences: he lost the respect of his teammates and performed poorly on the field. By May 2010, three years after being the most coveted college player, his NFL career was over, stemming from the sloth-like quality of laziness. Make no mistake, laziness is as dangerous as arrogance. It can quietly derail careers and be the leading barrier to a player reaching his full potential.

Pushing a lazy athlete into hard work is extremely difficult. Comfort often outweighs the perceived reward of effort. Your task as a coach is to help them understand the consequences of their habits and the impact on their future success.

CHAPTER 4

THE VORTEX

A VORTEX IS A powerful force that destroys its surroundings while pulling everything toward its center. A Vortex player does the same in a team setting—they hurt the team in order to draw attention to themselves. They care about stats over wins and will gladly choose individual accolades over team success. A good synonym for *vortex* is a black hole. No matter what name you use, their primary quality is destruction.

When asked if they care, they say yes—because in their mind, having talent and putting in hours of training somehow outweighs their selfishness. They've convinced themselves that caring gives them a right to a bad attitude when things don't go their way; throwing a fit is proof of passion, a necessary display to show they're invested. They believe they care about the team, when in reality, they only care about being *seen* as successful.

TRAITS

- Seeks individual success above all else
- Is unmoved by others' success
- Disappears when times get tough
- Deflects blame
- Is resistant to coaching
- Argues with officials

CARES ABOUT

Personal statistics, highlight plays, others' perceptions

DOESN'T CARE ABOUT

Team statistics, helping teammates succeed, receiving feedback

EXAMPLE

I once coached a highly talented young man who was identified early as a top player in the state. With that came a huge ego. He had a persistent attitude problem, resisted my coaching, and rarely smiled. Every time I thought I was making progress, he would regress. It felt like one step forward, two steps back.

Part of the challenge was his home environment. His parents believed he should always be the number one option in the lineup, even though he was already a starter. That expectation shaped his thinking. During a ten-game winning streak, he couldn't even crack a smile. His attitude created tension among teammates, building an undeniable strain in the locker room.

Two-thirds into the season, our best player suffered a season-ending injury. The talented young man with the attitude was thrust into a bigger role. He handled more shots, received more opportunities, and took center stage. Remarkably, we lost every game after that. Yet he was happier than ever. After thirty-point losses, he'd be high-fiving teammates, clapping while running down the court, and speaking like a leader. He was a Vortex in its purest form, thriving in chaos as his team fell apart around him.

CONVERSATIONS TO HAVE WITH A VORTEX

A Vortex discussion is the opposite of a Sloth discussion. Vortexes lack humility and self-reflection, making them extremely difficult to reach. They likely won't even acknowledge a problem. You can't change someone who refuses to recognize that change is needed. Think of the most difficult colleague you've tried to help for years without success. The issue isn't your guidance; it's that they don't see a problem.

Your primary goal with a Vortex is not to make them selfless but to raise their awareness. That's the starting line. They can't improve if they don't understand their impact.

One effective strategy is to show consequences in terms of their own performance:

> "When you complain about teammates during games, you're ultimately hurting yourself. They trust you less,

don't advocate for you when you struggle, and may perform worse, which affects you. Sometimes they even avoid passing you the ball, because they're tired of the way you act. Your attitude impacts *you* more than anyone else."

Deliver this message calmly and clearly. Avoid accusation. Don't beat around the bush, but avoid using a condemning tone. Your best chance is to appeal to their emotions and values.

Consider using a "compliment sandwich" when talking to a Vortex. A compliment sandwich places constructive feedback between two positive statements:

> "Hey, man, great shooting tonight. There were a few points where you talked back to me during the game, which isn't acceptable. I know you're capable of a positive presence this season."

This is far less threatening than simply yelling:

> "Stop talking back to me!"

While old-school coaches may see this as soft, it works. A Vortex defaults to defensiveness. Your tone should connect with their heart, not confront their ego.

HISTORICAL HIGHLIGHT

In the 2010s, the Pittsburgh Steelers were loaded with talent. Quarterback Ben Roethlisberger had already won a Super Bowl, and stars like Le'Veon Bell and Antonio Brown were among the best at their positions. Bell's patient, strategic running and Brown's explosive receiving made them must-watch television.

Yet despite their expertise, ego undermined the team. A group that was surely talented enough to win Super Bowls soon imploded from selfishness. Bell sat out multiple training camps and, eventually, the entire 2018 season due to contract disputes, limiting team cohesion and practice. Brown, meanwhile, created chaos in the locker room, refusing to mentor younger players and publicly criticizing teammates. When a young wide receiver received team MVP honors, Brown's ego interfered, and he expressed resentment, even on social media. He continued his detrimental behavior until the Steelers had no choice but to let him go. Players who could have been legends are instead known for controversy.

Vortex behavior is exemplified by small outbursts that escalate into a major implosion. A Vortex can be extremely talented, yet bad for your team.

The Steelers' "Killer B's" (Ben, Bell, and Brown) remain one of the greatest "what-ifs" in NFL history. Vortexes in prominent roles create inevitable tension, forcing coaches to choose between integrity and short-term wins. Integrity may cost games, but in the long term, it preserves culture, trust, and a foundation for sustainable success.

CHAPTER 5

THE ALLY

AN ALLY IS someone who fights on your side in a battle. They may not be the direct target of the enemy, but they choose to fight out of loyalty. An ally will support the cause regardless of their direct involvement. A team full of Allies fosters a strong culture.

An Ally works harder than a Vortex and cares more than a Sloth. When you combine hard work with care, you immediately have someone who can contribute to your team. An Ally is likely capable of playing a wide variety of minor to major roles. Think of an Ally as the engine that keeps the team moving smoothly. The tires and the vinyl are cool, but a vehicle can't move without the engine.

When questioned about their commitment to the team, they would readily affirm that they care, which would be truthful. Their effort is sufficient to affect competition, and their willingness to embrace any role reflects a meaningful level of selflessness.

TRAITS

- Prioritizes team success over personal accolades
- Lifts others up and encourages growth
- Is reliable under pressure
- Is coachable and receptive to feedback
- Leads by example without demanding attention

CARES ABOUT

Team success, helping teammates, learning, improving

DOESN'T CARE ABOUT

Personal glory, recognition, being in the spotlight

EXAMPLE

Throughout my years of coaching, I worked with two incredible players who were Heartbeats, which we'll discuss next. One was surrounded by Allies. The other was surrounded by Sloths and Vortexes. The player with a team of Allies set almost every individual and team school record. The other had a good career but didn't reach the apex. Interestingly, I believe the second player was slightly more talented and played a more important position. This demonstrates the value of an Ally: They help you get the most out of your team, including your star players.

Great talents sometimes think they don't have to do anything other than be great, but their teammates' skill and level of buy-in matter hugely, setting the floor and ceiling of the talent's career. That's the message we must deliver to our star players. It takes mentorship and intentional conversation to maximize a player's potential.

When your star athlete is surrounded by Allies, they are uplifted, encouraged, motivated, and supported with complementary talent. In contrast, Vortexes drain them, and Sloths don't work hard enough to be of any help. Getting your players to the third level of care is crucial to success.

My Allies consistently motivated the rest of the team by cheering on their teammates, whether they were playing well or not; committing to toughness, taking charges and rebounding; focusing on game prep; communicating well during practices and games; and having an overall positive attitude.

Think about why one country chooses to form an alliance with another country in a war. They care about the same mission or values as their ally. They believe the war is worth fighting and that the outcome matters. The same is true for your team. If you want your players to sign up as Allies, they need to care about your mission and values.

CONVERSATIONS TO HAVE WITH AN ALLY

An Ally needs encouragement, directly or indirectly. It's easy to overlook their contributions and assign credit to the Heartbeat. When you are interviewed after a big game, the reporter will often focus on your superstar. You may feel inclined to talk about them, but it's extremely important to mention Allies as well. Even if they weren't mentioned in the question, find a way to acknowledge and encourage them.

One time, my team barely squeaked out a win against a weak opponent. The reporter waited for me outside of the locker room as he always did after games. When he asked for my thoughts on the game, the coach in me told him that we played poorly and needed to improve. (My Heartbeat had fouled out, and the Allies had had to finish the game without him. They'd limped to the finish line, playing afraid.) I told the reporter that we couldn't fall apart just because our best player was missing.

A day later, I received a text from the mom of one of my best Ally players, a young man who did everything I asked of him and more. She felt it was unfair of me to imply that we had "sucked" without our star. I mulled it over and realized she had a point. I stand by my statement, but perhaps it should have stayed in the locker room. It's easy to feel like interviews are going to ESPN when, in reality, high school sports interviews are mostly read by players' families.

The moral of the story is that our Ally kids can often get overlooked and underappreciated, as we typically focus on the top and the bottom in terms of compliments and criticisms. As coaches, we need to be intentional about how we build them up; they've fully bought into our mission and should be acknowledged for that.

Conversations with an Ally can vary, but the goal is always the same: Make sure they know their efforts are seen and appreciated. Some days, you'll need to motivate them to improve. Other days, you'll need to spotlight the great things they're doing. Whatever you do, don't forget about them. If you go one day without complimenting the athletes who've wholeheartedly bought into your mission, you're making a mistake and missing an opportunity.

HISTORICAL HIGHLIGHT

What if I told you there was an NBA player who won seven championships, hit some of the biggest shots in finals history, and played sixteen seasons, yet the average fan doesn't know who he is? That player exists—his name is Robert Horry.

Horry played for the Rockets, Lakers, and Spurs. Since the adoption of the three-point line in 1979, Horry holds the NBA record for the player with the most championship wins— seven. He earned the nickname "Big Shot Bob" for his uncanny ability to make clutch shots in playoff games. He was never named to an all-star team and never averaged more than twelve points per season. His statistics wouldn't stand out, and his basketball card isn't commonly preserved. Yet he is considered one of the most import- ant NBA players in league history.

His clutch 3-pointers helped Hakeem Olajuwon, Clyde Drexler, Shaquille O'Neal, Kobe Bryant, Tim Duncan, and David Robinson win championships. In 1995, he hit a game-clinching 3-pointer against the Spurs. In 2002, he kept the Lakers alive with a buzzer-beating 3-pointer. In the 2005 championship, he scored 21 points in the fourth quarter and made a critical 3-pointer with five seconds left to seal the win. He consistently showed up when his team needed him.

In every sport, there comes a time when a role player is thrust into a do-or-die scenario. It's your job to ensure they're ready when that moment arrives.

Despite his playoff resume, Horry didn't demand more minutes, fame, or money. He owned his role as an Ally. He played whatever his team needed and stayed ready, two qualities essential for a good Ally.

This is one of the hardest roles on a team. Ego can easily override humility, but a true Ally embraces a role that doesn't come with fame. Allies and star players alike do the same painful and time-consuming workouts, but only star players receive awards and recognition. The Hall of Famers that Robert Horry played alongside needed Allies to win. Without them, even all-time greats like Charles Barkley, Chris Paul, and Steve Nash would have gone ringless.

It's crucial that Allies know they are as important as superstars. They are more than helpful—they're necessary. In every sport, there comes a time when a role player is thrust into a do-or-die scenario. It's your job to ensure they're ready when that moment arrives.

CHAPTER 6

THE HEARTBEAT

YOUR HEARTBEAT IS what gives life to your body. Without it, you would die. What's interesting about the heart is that every single body part depends on it to pump blood. With every beat, blood fuels the entire organism.

In his book *Leading with the Heart*, Hall of Fame coach Mike Krzyzewski stated that he identified the player who would be the heartbeat in every one of his teams.[2] He leaned on this player to provide the majority of peer leadership.

This player needs to be highly skilled and care about the entire team more than themselves. Some might question why the leader needs to be skilled, as leadership is a mentality, not a physical trait. But if you're not skilled, you won't be in a position to lead from the court or field. No one can lead their teammates in crunch time from the bench. Your skill also garners influence, which puts you in a position to lead well. The Heartbeat is willing to do whatever it takes to win a game. Just as the human body needs a heartbeat, so does the team.

The difference between a Heartbeat player and an Ally player is the attention they give to the parts of a team nobody notices. While an Ally works hard and shows up for their role, a Heartbeat player steps into the spaces between the lines. They offer encouragement when a teammate is struggling, challenge a peer who's coasting, and put in the quiet, relentless effort to help others grow. They check in with coaches, absorb feedback, and act as the glue that holds the team together. More than their talent, effort, and selflessness, they are the pulse that keeps the team alive.

TRAITS

- Leads by example
- Is highly skilled
- Finds ways to contribute to success outside of the expected norms
- Empathizes with everyone in the room
- Galvanizes people around the mission
- Is trustworthy
- Has integrity
- Isn't judgmental

CARES ABOUT

Every player and coach on the team, putting in "extra mile" work, the details

DOESN'T CARE ABOUT

Not getting the glory, drama

EXAMPLE

One of the best players I ever coached entered a game against a rival 36 points shy of the elusive 1,000-point mark. In high school basketball, that's a crowning individual achievement. To score 1,000 points, you either have to play varsity all four years or be an exceptionally high-volume scorer for two to three years. Either way, reaching the 1,000-point club requires incredible skill. There's a reason why large plaques in high school gyms honor those who achieve this feat. This player was lightning quick, and his first step made it impossible for defenders to stay in front of him.

We didn't anticipate him scoring 36 points in that game, but as the game progressed, he got closer and closer. When he hit 30 points, I wondered, "How do we go about this?" Typically, a coach would call easy plays or allow him extra shots. When he reached the mark, the coach would call a timeout and allow the fans to give him an ovation. But this was a game we had to win. We couldn't afford trick plays or an extra timeout. We had to let it unfold and hope for the best.

Tied up, we headed into overtime. Incredibly, he reached 34 points and was a basket away from 1,000. With ten seconds left, he had the ball while we were down by one. What happened next shows why this kid was the clear choice for our Heartbeat. The defender came at him hard. He drove past as he always did, entered the lane, side-stepped, and jumped. As the second defender approached, rather than take the shot for himself, as he had hundreds of times before, he passed to a teammate, who scored at the buzzer. We won in exhilarating fashion.

Rather than having the athletic moment of a lifetime, scoring his 1,000th point on a game-winner versus a rival, he chose his team over himself. Additionally, he gave his teammate invaluable confidence that bled into the next few games. That's what a Heartbeat does. They always do what's best for the team.

As noted earlier, it's important that a Heartbeat is a skilled athlete. Typically, coaches don't emphasize the obvious: You can't have a Heartbeat who doesn't play in the game. You can't have a Heartbeat subbed out in key moments. You can't have a Heartbeat you don't trust.

A Heartbeat and a leader are not the same. Anyone can be a leader, but to be the Heartbeat of a team, you must have the skill to back it up, along with an intense passion for the greater good of the team.

CONVERSATIONS TO HAVE WITH A HEARTBEAT

The Heartbeat can typically handle coach-like conversations. They can receive the full truth, won't take criticism personally, and won't let praise inflate their ego. If you want them to be a messenger in the locker room, they need full information. Often, a Heartbeat's voice is more effective than a coach's. Quite frankly, a team will respect a peer more than an adult. I could tell my team to attend summer workouts, and about half would listen. If it came from a peer, most would comply. Teens often think adults are unreasonable, so sometimes the message needs to come from the Heartbeat.

In professional sports, the "players-only meeting" is a popular concept. When a season is spiraling, players meet without coaches to discuss opinions freely. Not all players trust the coaches. Many fans don't realize that coaches often suggest these meetings to the captains. The meetings aren't insurrections; the staff knows about them and even schedules them, trusting the Heartbeats to lead and resolve issues.

In high school sports, athletes aren't fully mature. There's no professional forum for them to express thoughts clearly. But they do hold informal "players-only" discussions daily in the locker room after practices and games, usually initiated by the leaders.

A conversation you should have with your Heartbeat involves teaching them how to navigate these moments: bring the team together, don't divide, stay calm unless necessary to ignite energy, transmit core values, stick to the game plan, allow others to speak, and prevent dissension. You're essentially giving them leadership training. Companies spend millions annually on leadership development, and teenagers deserve it too.

I recommend a weekly sit-down with your Heartbeat to discuss progress and struggles. Being on the same page is critical. For me, it was after home games. I had an office in the locker room. After he cleaned up and players cleared out, he'd come in, and we'd share everything about the game: the good, the bad, and the ugly. We were both open to suggestions. It was important for me and my leader to be united. I believe teams can sense disunity, which leads to doubt. These conversations were critical. Sometimes it was five minutes, sometimes an hour. We didn't rush. Every year, my Heartbeat and I did the same thing. Consistency is key.

HISTORICAL HIGHLIGHT

In 1980, in Lake Placid, New York, perhaps the greatest sports underdog story of all time occurred. At a time when USA hockey was an afterthought and the Russians dominated the sport, no one expected the US team to win. Most of us know the ending, as they made it into one of the best sports movies of all time. The United States hockey team shocked the world by beating the Soviets 4–3. *Sports Illustrated* named this the top sports moment of the twentieth century.

But what doesn't get talked about enough is Mike Eruzione. Eruzione was the captain of this miracle-performing hockey squad. The players were not professionals; they were college kids hoping to prove themselves. In today's landscape, professionals typically represent countries in international play. In the 1980s, amateurs filled the roster. This came with a lack of maturity. These young men were expected to take on perhaps the greatest responsibility of all: representing their country. They had to grow up fast and assume leadership qualities we'd expect from thirty-year-olds.

There was an open seat for someone to claim the Heartbeat's seat, a seat that came with insurmountable pressure. You know what they say: Heavy is the head that wears the crown.

Eruzione was not the most skilled player on Team USA. He was known for grit, work ethic, and the ability to unite people. Most importantly, he bought into Coach Herb Brooks' vision. He checked every box to qualify as the Heartbeat. He knew Coach would push them hard and that success required pushing their bodies to the limit. Eruzione was the glue that held the team together when they were tired, angry, or discouraged. Training was grueling. Players could have quit or turned on Coach Brooks, but they didn't.

In the game versus the Soviets, tied 3–3 with ten minutes left, Eruzione scored the go-ahead goal, perhaps the greatest single play in sports history. Do you know what his response was? Immediately after, he said, "There's still ten minutes left!

Play your game!" That's unbelievable! His focus was always on what the team needed to succeed. The Heartbeat never seeks individual glory; they push for team greatness.

CHAPTER 7

LEVELS OF CARE RECAP

THE LEVELS OF care are derived from two factors: selflessness and work ethic.

Selflessness is valuing others above yourself. It goes against social media culture. It's not about being in the spotlight or having your name called; it's caring about the greater good of the team more than your own success.

Work ethic is doing what it takes to excel. Weightlifting, film study, and skill work all count. It's doing one more rep than required, showing up when it's not mandatory, and volunteering for extra work in drills.

By plotting selflessness and work ethic on a chart, we can see how the four levels of care are determined.

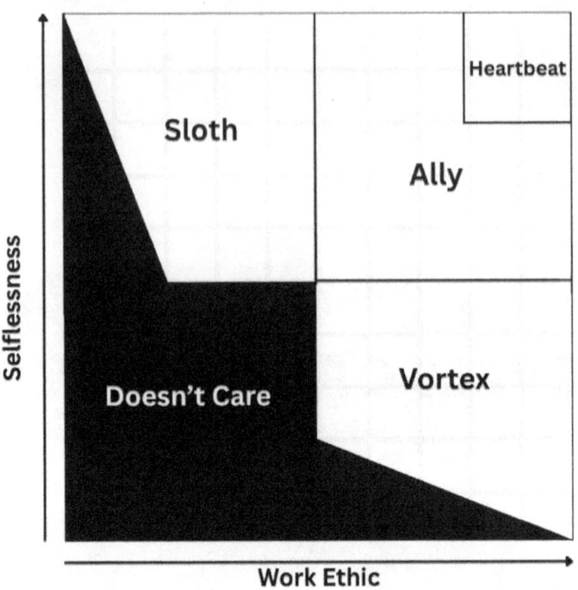

HEARTBEAT

A team's Heartbeat should be at least 8/10 in both work ethic and selflessness. Some seasons, you won't have anyone at this level, but don't just assign the role by default. Either develop someone to reach it or find another way to fill the gap. Rarely, you may have multiple Heartbeats, but avoid too many cooks in the kitchen. Occasionally, two players may share leadership duties, but only if the situation demands it.

ALLY

To be an Ally, a player must be at least 5/10 in both selflessness and work ethic. To put it simply, they care more often than they don't. Allies won't be perfect. Some days they'll be off, and that's normal. You might need a motivational chat here and there, but a true Ally will rise to the challenge and fix it.

SLOTH VS. VORTEX

A Sloth and a Vortex are opposites. Each shows strength in one area, work ethic or selflessness, but lacks the other. A Vortex may be skilled, but they're volatile; eventually, their fuse will ignite. A Sloth, on the other hand, rarely explodes. You're trying to light their fuse.

THE BOTTOM LINE

If a player can't show both selflessness and work ethic at least half the time, they don't care. You can build one skill but rarely both, because improving one requires the other.

APPLICATION

Discuss the four levels of care with your team. Make sure they understand what authentic care for the team looks like.

Ask them to rank themselves and the team according to the following categories, from 1 (lowest) to 10 (highest).

- Individual work ethic
- Individual selflessness
- Team work ethic
- Team selflessness

I recommend keeping the individual rankings private or anonymous; otherwise players will just write what sounds good. But share how each player ranked the team, then ask players for their thoughts on the team rankings.

1. Are they accurate?
2. What did you take into account as you decided on a number?

3. What are some things we can do to improve our work ethic?
4. What are some things we can do to improve our selflessness?

CHAPTER 8

LEVELING UP

I T WOULD BE incredibly unfair to discuss all the levels at which someone cares about the team without also discussing ways to improve those levels. Think about team culture-building like the weight room. The beginning is awkward and uncomfortable. It might take a while to see results. After a long period of consistency, you'll start to notice progress. Once you see results, you become more confident and seek out newer and better ways to continue improving. Growth then becomes exponential.

Beginning these conversations can also be very awkward. Being vulnerable is hard. Everything a coach asks of a team he or she must also do personally. You can't ask kids to engage in self-reflection without doing it yourself. At the start, you will need to model the behavior: tell your team what you're working on and what your insecurities

You can't ask kids to engage in self-reflection without doing it yourself.

are. Once they see your staff demonstrating vulnerability, they'll begin to feel more comfortable and start mimicking that behavior.

Scheduling team culture time into your practice schedule is vital. It's no different than scheduling a team lift or a game film study session. If it's important, make time for it. You wouldn't expect your team to get stronger without scheduled weight room time. Neither will team culture improve without time and effort.

I found it successful to prioritize team culture meetings early in the season. For the first two weeks, I scheduled fifteen-minute discussions every day, either before or after practice. Some years, we read books together, such as *The Energy Bus* by Jon Gordon.[3] Other years, I mapped out a plan based on my team's strengths and weaknesses.

A strong framework for building team culture usually follows a structure that includes the following:

- Rules
- Goal setting
- Communication

RULES

Rules should be established early and reinforced often. Never compromise on your standards. Don't drag out the process either; lay out your expectations clearly from day one. Avoid gray areas; everything should be black and white, right or wrong. Thoroughness is the name of the game. Make sure your rules cover not only behavior during team activities but also conduct in school and in the community. Players represent your team everywhere they go.

There's nothing worse for a coach than finding out that a player has become ineligible because of grades or behavior. We often learn things the hard way, and I was no exception. During my first season as a varsity coach, the day before tryouts, I was notified that one of my top players would miss half the season after being caught on video smoking at a party. Then, midway through the year, my senior guard was ruled ineligible because of poor grades. It was a mess. I had naively thought my job was limited to influencing and shaping behavior in the locker room and on the court. I couldn't have been more wrong.

Making the rules and expectations explicitly clear at the beginning of your season is integral to establishing a positive team culture.

GOAL SETTING

Goals are the road map to any successful season. They keep players motivated, give practices purpose, and help everyone measure progress beyond wins and losses. Performance is important, but the heart of your goal setting is to build a shared vision. When your players buy into common goals, they start playing for something bigger than themselves. This mindset shift turns a group of individuals into a team. Setting both individual and team goals is crucial at the start of every season—they set the tone for how your players will think, act, and grow.

Players often mistake goals for anything statistical. Without guidance, they'll write things like "10 wins," "50 percent shooting," or ".300 batting average." But numbers only tell part of the story. Our job, as coaches, is to push and inspire our players to look deeper—to set goals that develop their character and work ethic. Those are the goals that build habits, and habits determine who they become as athletes and people.

Have players write down personal goals along with their performance-based goals. For example:

- Get to practice early once a week to get extra shots up
- Stretch every morning before school
- Refrain from talking back to coaches when I get subbed out

These goals might seem small, but they add up. They teach accountability, discipline, and humility. When players begin to see improvement in these areas, the wins tend to follow naturally.

Another key aspect of goal setting is sharing them as a team. It's not enough for players to write them down and keep them private. How can teammates encourage and hold each other accountable if they don't know what everyone is working toward? Sharing individual goals builds connection and creates a sense of ownership within the team.

There are several ways to do this. You can have players pass their goals to the person on their right and read each other's goals aloud to the group. It will probably feel uncomfortable at first, but as well as building vulnerability and trust, it sends a signal that everyone is in this together.

Another idea is for players to write their goals on index cards and tape them up in the locker room, either on a wall or directly on their lockers. Seeing those goals every day is a powerful reminder of the commitments they've made. You can even take it a step further by creating a team "word wall." Write down the goals that appear most often and use them to build an official team goal sheet for the season.

Whatever processes you use, do it with intentionality. You're building a foundation for your culture. When players learn how to set meaningful goals, support each other, and take ownership of their growth, they stop playing for approval and start playing with purpose. And that's when something special happens.

COMMUNICATION

Every coach needs to address a few key aspects of communication early on: universal language, leadership, and character building.

UNIVERSAL LANGUAGE

Every team needs a shared vocabulary. Introduce concepts and terms like *Sloth, Vortex, Ally,* and *Heartbeat*—the language of this book. Once your players understand these ideas, they'll start using the same words and images to describe behavior and culture. When everyone speaks the same language, it becomes easier to communicate expectations, correct issues, and celebrate growth.

LEADERSHIP

Decide early how you'll structure leadership on your team. Will you have captains, leadership committees, or rotating leaders? Whatever you choose, make sure your players understand the *why* behind it and that leadership involves responsibility and setting an example. Establish for your players what leadership should look like and that they will earn it through consistency and character.

CHARACTER-BUILDING LESSONS

Don't leave character development to chance. Choose topics that align with your vision for the team—work ethic, attitude, trust, accountability, and so on. Weave these lessons into practices, meetings, and everyday conversations. Teams that excel work on who they are becoming together. The application questions in this book provide practical ways to engage your team.

Starting the season the right way is crucial to long-term success. It's far easier to build strong habits from day one than to realize mid-season that something's missing and try to fix it on the fly. The early days of the season lay the groundwork for everything that follows.

In the next chapters, we'll walk through specific strategies you can use to level up your team—from apathy to alignment, from a group of individuals to a unified organism.

APPLICATION

1. Create a list of non-negotiables for behavior on your team, in school, and in the community. Display the list prominently in your locker room.
2. Develop a system for keeping track of your players' goals throughout the season. Establish check-ins with your athletes in order to discuss progress.
3. Have your entire team write down three goals for the team at the beginning of the season—goals can be statistical or character-based. Read them aloud. Consolidate these ideas to a list of five goals for your team to strive for throughout the season.
4. Find a book to read through this season or off-season with your team and staff. Share what you're learning with each other.
5. Make a list of communication expectations for your program.

6. Pick one virtue to discuss per week for the first month of your season. That discussion should be planned out and intentional. Each day of the week you should reiterate the virtue with a new anecdote or application in practice.

7. Think about some habits that you want to be established in the first week of the season.

CAPTAINCY

MY FIRST YEAR as a head coach, I did what everyone does: I named team captains. The issue? The talent on the team was mostly in the underclassmen, and there's an unspoken rule that the best players are named captains. The clear choice was a sophomore, but my seniors weren't going to accept a younger peer leading them.

I've found that this mindset—that the older players should automatically be the leaders—often comes from the parents. The number one pushback I faced as a head coach was from parents of seniors upset that freshmen and sophomores were playing over their sons. It didn't stop there. The parents resisted younger players being included in anything their seniors weren't given, whether it was leadership roles, team responsibilities, or a post on social media. They struggled to accept my simple principle: The best players play, regardless of age. The best leaders lead, regardless of age.

The team ended up voting two seniors as the captains, which didn't sit well with the younger guys. I had a hard time watching this unfold—the pettiness of the veteran players, the whining of the younger players. That first week thrust me into the deep end of team culture management. I learned right away, coaching is problem-solving more than planning the X's and O's of the strategy. I had to nip this in the bud before it spiraled into a season-long issue.

Coaches make a common mistake: sweeping problems under the rug, especially those they view as minor or irrational. In the moment, it may seem like a waste of energy. Surely there are bigger things to focus on. But you need to think ahead. Certain issues, like emerging bitterness between players, can escalate into major problems. Even if a problem seems small in the moment, it demands your immediate attention—or you risk paying the price later.

After the vote, the players cleared out. I watched as they all walked out of the room in their cliques. One remained. He was emotional. A sophomore, he was clearly our best player and hardest worker. He didn't think it was fair that the older guys had snubbed him as the team captain for two guys who didn't deserve it. I told him to go home and come back the next day with a written explanation of why being a captain was important to him. I asked him to include an explanation of what a captain does, along with what he felt he couldn't do now because he wasn't a captain. I think it's better to allow kids time to think rather than demand an answer on the spot. He went off, he hung low, and he came back the next day.

The next morning, before school started, he walked into my office, and said, "I know why you asked me to do that. When I thought about it, I couldn't figure out why being a captain matters. I'm not even sure what they do." I was proud of him; he put effort into thinking about the topic. And he was correct. When you really think about it, a captain is just a name.

I did some thinking that night as well: *It's your first year as a head coach. You can either mirror the coaches you've seen or forge your own path. You don't have to fit a mold. Do what you believe in. Set the tone right now—don't wait.*

I had watched other programs where captains were chosen strictly based on talent, often creating resentment and apathy among players who weren't chosen. Practices felt like a hierarchy, and quiet leaders didn't step up because the label wasn't theirs to claim.

I wanted to avoid that trap. Leadership isn't something you assign; it's something that emerges when the environment allows it to. The process had revealed that titles are secondary to character, effort, and influence. It was a living example of how awareness, accountability, and opportunity shape team chemistry.

Leadership isn't something you assign; it's something that emerges when the environment allows it to.

I knew what I needed to do. Before practice the next day, I told my team we were not going to have captains. I explained:

"The issue with having a labeled captain is that it actually suppresses leadership. If we want an atmosphere where everyone can be leaders, there has to be the ability to lead. If I named two guys as captains, that means thirteen others would tap out of the race to develop leadership skills. The only thing a captain really does is shake hands before a game. Who cares? If you need a title to lead, then you're not truly leading. Part of being a leader is doing the hard things without recognition or reward. I want real leaders on this team—I'm not interested in posers. Because of that, we will not be naming captains. The rest will work itself out."

After that incident, I decided that I wasn't interested in ever messing with the process of selecting team captains. The negative outcomes far outweighed the positive. That season, and every season after, I rotated the pre-game captains. In basketball, the captains miss out on warm-up time. Two of the fifteen minutes are taken up by a pointless rules meeting with the refs (sorry, we all know the rules; nothing necessary happens in these meetings). When I realized this, I made the bench guys handle the pre-game meeting. It gave my starters precious time to get ready for the game. What's funny is that parents complimented me for being "inclusive," because, to them, I was giving the spotlight to the kids not playing. Which wasn't true, but I never told them that. You take parent points when you can get them.

Not having labeled captains didn't matter. The leaders rose up and led. The rest of the team followed. I unlocked something I found to be extremely valuable. I was encouraged when I found out that professional teams, like the Green Bay Packers, had started doing the same thing. Leaders will lead regardless of the situation; it's innately in their blood. The worst thing you can do is take your leaders out of the race because of an arbitrary, outdated process.

I found the levels of care concept valuable in this process. The Heartbeat of the team was never announced or named; it happened naturally. As the true leader rose up, we embraced them and let nature take its course.

This story speaks directly to the foundations of team chemistry. When the environment allows leadership to emerge naturally, players step up in ways that benefit not only themselves but the entire group. Giving players labels and titles doesn't create leaders, but culture and opportunity do. By focusing on aware-ness, addressing issues early, and giving everyone the chance to contribute, you build a team where influence flows from effort, character, and commitment, unrelated to age or title. Chemistry is cultivated and rooted in creating a space where leadership, respect, and accountability thrive organically.

As you develop this kind of culture, you'll witness a group of individuals transforming into a high-performing, cohesive team, where every heart in the locker room is invested in the mission.

This concept raises a much bigger question: which schematic decisions, rules, expectations, drills, or workouts are outdated—kept alive not because they work, but because they've always been done or because someone else is doing them? You know exactly what I'm talking about: procedures that if you were forced to explain them, you'd struggle to justify. The warm-up you ran because you did it in high school, the dress code enforced a decade ago, the lifting program passed down like an heirloom. We can't operate out of fear of change or cling to tradition simply because it feels safe. We'll dive deeper into this in chapter 15.

If you find yourself stuck in a rut, evaluate every procedure and routine the way I had to evaluate my captaincy dilemma. More than slowing progress, rigid, outdated systems can breed jealousy, bitterness, and distrust. They fracture your staff and leave your players resentful of the person in charge. And how does this affect *care*? Simple, if you don't genuinely believe in what you're doing, why should they? When you continue practices that clearly don't work, your players will question your competence. They're smart. They see it. And once doubt creeps in, buy-in disappears.

The issue at stake in this chapter is courage. The courage to question tradition, disrupt comfortable systems, and trust that genuine leadership doesn't need a label to exist. Care shows up when a coach is willing to protect the culture regardless of whether it's inconvenient or unpopular. Titles and traditions don't build strong teams; it takes intentional leadership. As you intentionally show you care and build the right environment, the right people always rise to the surface.

APPLICATION

1. Which athletes in your program have shown leadership potential? Make a list.
2. What criteria are you looking for when trying to identify team leaders?
3. In what ways can you encourage those athletes to step into leadership responsibilities?
4. In what ways are you allowing room for any athlete in your program to step up in leadership?
5. Are your captain procedures empty gestures, or do you have a clear purpose for the tasks they perform?
6. Do you have a set of standards that your leaders need to live up to? If not, create a list.
7. Do your leaders allow others on the team to grow in their leadership? Do they mentor the younger players to prepare them for leadership? If not, how can you give them opportunities in this area?
8. If your players mirrored your habits and attitude, what kind of leaders would they be?

CHAPTER 10

AWARENESS

ONE YEAR, MY locker room was full of Vortexes. Every day felt like an uphill battle. I spent the bulk of most halftimes discussing body language and attitude. I was doing more counseling than coaching! Coaching is like that. Some years, you'll have extremely coachable teams; other years, you'd prefer a colonoscopy to getting through five months with your group. If you're coaching middle or high school, you more than likely have no say in which students try out for your team. Don't waste time complaining—brushing off an entire season because you're frustrated is not an option.

When you have difficult teams, it's time to dig deep. You get paid to be a coach, but coaching isn't all you do. You're a mentor, an advocate, an advisor. That's the part society misses. People assume you just need to figure out how to get your offense and defense (or whatever your sport involves) to work well. But

> You get paid to be a coach, but coaching isn't all you do.

your job is actually to determine how to get your entire locker room on board so that they *care* about the mission. As the old adage goes, they won't care how much you know until they know how much you care.

That year with my team of Vortexes was unlike any other. I couldn't figure it out. No matter how many lectures I delivered on behavioral dos and don'ts, I couldn't move the needle. I prided myself on being a culture expert—it was my thing. But far from improving, this group's issues were getting worse. It felt like I was trying to cook without all the ingredients.

One day, I had had enough. I canceled practice and sent everyone to the locker room. As they waited, I paced the hallway outside (when you're angry, give yourself time to cool down before responding). I had an idea. On the whiteboard I drew a diagram with four quadrants. The axes were "works hard" and "coachable" (this later inspired the idea behind the levels of care).

The bottom left quadrant was "not coachable and doesn't work hard." The term I associated with this was *toxic*. If you couldn't work hard or support the team, you were no good to us and would fit in this quadrant.

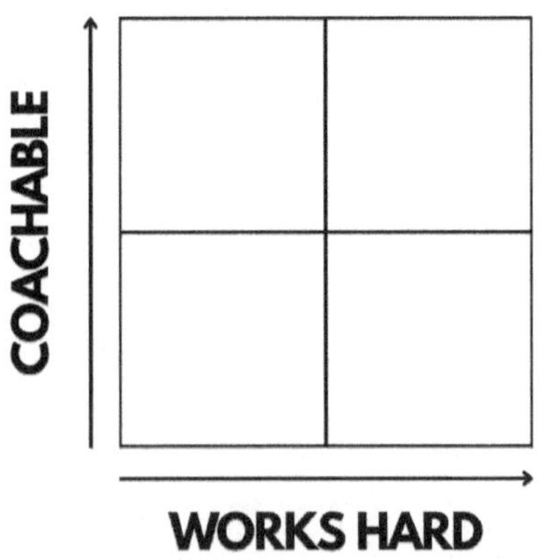

The upper left was "coachable but doesn't work hard"—the *freeloader*, a player who is along for the ride but not doing any work. The first level of care, *the Sloth*, is similar. If they skipped summer workouts or missed small things like touching the line during sprints, they belonged in the *freeloader* quadrant.

The bottom right was "works hard but isn't coachable." The term I associated with this was *energy vampire*, a concept from Jon Gordon's leadership training. He says, "I call the people who drain your energy Energy Vampires, and they will suck the energy out of life and your vision and goals if you let them."[4] My second level, *the Vortex*, falls under this category. They suck the energy out of the room everywhere they go. Players who talk back to coaches, complain frequently, shake their head when being subbed out, and argue with referees would be in this box. Every player on my team that year should've put themselves here.

The top right represented the ideal player: someone who works hard and rarely shows moments of character flaw. No one from this team was close to being in the upper right quadrant.

I asked every player to walk up and write their initials where they thought they fit. I stepped aside for several minutes while they thought about it and made their mark on the board. I was expecting to return to a smattering of initials in each box and wondered how I'd address each one. But I was shocked when I saw the results.

Every single player had put themselves in the top right! They all viewed themselves as hard workers and coachable, though not a single one belonged there. It hit me like a brick to the face: the problem wasn't improving because they were oblivious to the problem. You can't help someone who thinks they don't have a problem. Awareness is the key to improvement. Your team won't improve unless they're *aware* of a problem.

I explained to my players that they couldn't claim to be hard workers if they took plays off, skipped off-season workouts, or jogged during sprints. Further, they couldn't claim to be coachable if they'd ever argued with an instruction or shaken their heads when being subbed out of a game. They looked at me as if I had told them Santa wasn't real. They couldn't believe they might not be the most pleasant players to coach.

You can't help someone who thinks they don't have a problem.

You might be wondering, "Hunter, didn't you have conversations like this with them before it came to this?" Yes, I did, in ways that proved ineffective. The error in my previous attempts was that I didn't present it in a way that was obvious to them. I gave them gray areas. Anyone can make excuses in a gray area. With black and white, there are no excuses. You either do it, or you don't.

In that moment, I knew we had to have a vulnerable conversation and could not leave until every one of us knew what problem we needed to fix. As a coach, you should always model the behavior you're looking for, so I started with myself. I told them ways I'd come up short—times where my anger had gotten the better of me, when I'd gone too far yelling at an official. I expressed regret and the awareness that there was a behavior that I needed to fix.

Then I moved on to them. I listed all the ways that they'd been difficult to coach. I shared, respectfully, that up to that point I'd had a miserable season. I didn't look forward to coming in to coach like I used to. I made it clear that their lack of coachability and constant attitude issues made my job incredibly difficult. The last question I asked them was "If I left tomorrow, why would someone else want to come coach you?" They couldn't answer it. They sat quietly and stared into my eyes. It hit them. They had a major problem to address.

Coaches, you have to make them aware, and that requires a real and vulnerable conversation. Honestly, it might have an even greater impact when it comes from the Heartbeat of the team rather than the coaches. There's a time and a place for everything. It's on the leaders of the team, both coaches and players, to kick off improvement by building awareness.

Think of it like a practice plan. You don't walk into practice without a plan, simply *hoping* to get better that day. No, you have a well-thought-out plan based on your team's strengths and weaknesses. Your team culture needs a practice plan too. How will you address it? Who will deliver the message? How will you make them aware that there's a problem? You might have to cancel practice and sacrifice a couple of hours to make it clear that this is important. Just like a bad drill, you might have to abandon something that doesn't work the way you expected. As the leader of the team, it's on you not to give up on this mission. It's on you to set a standard of excellence. If it's a priority to you, you'll make time and space for it.

Something to keep in mind as you deal with the frustrations of feeling that the players on your team are overly difficult and wasting your time: they weren't born this way. Something influenced their lack of awareness, lack of work ethic, or lack of selflessness. It can come from scars in the form of overbearing parents. It can develop from an abusive coach. It could even stem from sibling pressures. After all, these kids are just that—kids.

There will be times when you want to throw your fist through a wall because you're pouring into someone who just isn't improving. It might be that the message they're hearing at home is completely opposite to yours. You're asking them to have a better attitude and support their teammates, but their parents may be yelling at them to be more selfish and demand more playing time. There's no certified solution in these situations. Keep attempting to win their hearts.

> Coaching difficult teams isn't about surviving the season; it's about shaping people who don't yet realize who they can become.

You should be able to sleep fine at night knowing that you're attempting to help them and trying to invest in them. You can't control what their background or home environment is. I find it helpful to step back and recenter my mind around the idea that they're not a bad person; they're just making bad decisions.

At the end of the day, coaching difficult teams isn't about surviving the season; it's about shaping people who don't yet realize who they can become. You won't fix every attitude, you won't reach every kid, and you won't see every breakthrough you hoped for. But awareness, vulnerability, and consistency give you a fighting chance.

Some players will surprise you, others will frustrate you, and a few may never come around. Still, your job is to keep showing up with clarity, compassion, and conviction.

Culture doesn't change because you lecture louder but because you lead with purpose. When it feels like you're coaching in a storm, remember this: the work you're doing isn't wasted. You're planting seeds that may not grow today, but one day, those same kids will remember the standard you held them to—and they'll be better for it.

APPLICATION

1. What poor habits or behaviors have you "let go" in past seasons that you need to make your team aware of this season?
2. Does every player on your team know what their areas for improvement are? What "gray areas" do you unintentionally create that allow excuses to form?
3. How comfortable are you with shifting between coach, mentor, and counselor? Which role do you naturally avoid? How can you improve at that role?
4. Where do you think most of your players would place themselves if they completed the four-quadrant exercise today—and where would *you* place them? Discuss with your staff.
5. What is one cultural issue that you've been hoping will fix itself but actually needs an intentional intervention?
6. What are your strengths in the area of awareness? Make a list.
7. What your weaknesses in the area of awareness? Make a list.

CHAPTER 11

ACCOUNTABILITY

AWARENESS IS JUST the beginning. Once your team knows there's a problem, the next step is accountability. Without it, goals are meaningless. Imagine you set a goal of ten wins for the season. Halfway through, you only have two wins. You wouldn't just shrug your shoulders; you'd evaluate, adjust, and hold people accountable. You'd address inefficiencies and tell players exactly what they need to do. You might even give someone else a chance to step into a role where a player was performing poorly. You'd push your coaches to step up and find solutions.

Team culture goals are just as important as statistical goals. You can't set them once and never revisit them. How many of you share your expectations the first week of the season and then never bring them up again? Too often, this is the case.

Accountability takes integrity from the one holding others accountable. It requires delicate and vulnerable conversations—and impartiality. If you harbor resentful feelings toward the person, you may veer into harsh criticism. If you're fond of the person, you may struggle to be critical.

In one of my Bible studies with a group of high-achieving coaches in town, a crucial point surfaced when we discussed discipline: the balance of grace and truth. Being able to operate out of both is essential in leadership. A strong leader must show mercy and patience when mistakes are made yet also deliver honest, necessary criticism when it's required. As humans, we tend to default to one extreme or the other. Some lean heavily on grace, to the point of becoming pushovers. Others rely almost exclusively on harsh truth-telling, sometimes forgetting compassion in the process. While each approach has its place in certain scenarios, coaches need to be skilled in both. True leadership demands the ability to be merciful when appropriate and firm when necessary.

Excessive grace leads to a team doing whatever they want, whenever they want. The result is a coach who avoids confronting poor behavior and a team that essentially runs the show. Players show up late, become disrespectful, practice sloppy habits, and are often quarrelsome. On the other hand, excessive truth, delivering criticism without compassion, creates a team that's afraid of their coach. The culture becomes one of fear and stress rather than joy and passion. Kids start quitting, and those who remain tiptoe around you, making genuine connection impossible.

Accountability is most effective in an environment of psychological safety, where players know they can speak up, make mistakes, and be honest without fear of humiliation or punishment. When players feel safe, they are far more likely to accept correction, because they trust that the correction is for their growth, not their shame. But in a team that lacks psychological safety, even the smallest criticism feels like an attack. Players shut down, deflect, or hide their mistakes. Accountability becomes the enemy rather than a gift. Coaches must build a culture where truth can be spoken without inducing fear and grace can be given without loss of standards.

During the study time with local coaches, a question was asked to the group: *How can we show more grace to our athletes when they need it?* One man in the group, an athletic trainer who'd been on the job for many years, added, "I have a comment to add from a non-coach perspective. It seems to me, as an outsider, that kids with more talent get a longer leash. Is that something you guys recognize?" The room went quiet—we knew it was true. We seem to give more grace to players with more talent, and more truth to players who don't offer us talent. Why? The answer is obvious: disciplining the talent can hurt us far more as a team than when we discipline a lesser player. For example, if a talented player is suspended from a game, it's harder to win without their skillset. Our ego overrides our logic. That's one reason accountability is hard in sports. It's incredibly difficult to rationalize hurting your chances of winning to maintain order.

Coaches are judged by wins and losses. Some will disagree, but it's true. At some point in your coaching career, you'll be forced to answer the question *How much is a win worth?* When that time comes, the decision will be harder than you think. Accountability is a fickle beast. It can hurt you in the short term but be the best thing for your team in the long term. If your team truly desires to be great, discomfort is required.

I struggled with punishing players that left my team vulnerable to a loss. My competitive nature blinded my ability to see the bigger picture. I was so afraid of losing that it was easy for me to turn a blind eye to infractions that I knew were important to address. I would find ways to talk myself into letting a behavior in a key player slide so I could keep them in a game. What I didn't see as I relished my short-cut victory was that I was setting up bad habits for the rest of the year.

If I could go back and have my career again, that's the number one thing I would change. I wouldn't treat winning as the only thing that mattered. The funny thing is, now that I'm onto a new career, not a single person in my orbit cares whether I won that third conference game in December that pushed us up in the standings. I'm not sure that the players even remember it. But the life lessons have lasted forever. In hindsight, it should have been an easy decision.

Coaches often feel the pull of cognitive dissonance—the mental discomfort that comes when our actions don't match our values. We say culture matters more than winning, but in the heat of competition, we knowingly let things that violate our standards slide. Instead of confronting the behavior, we quiet the discomfort by rationalizing it: *It's just one time,* or *We need him tonight.*

Dissonance doesn't disappear; it quietly shapes your team's identity. When your players see you compromising your own values, they learn that standards are flexible. Accountability isn't just correcting your team; it's also refusing to negotiate with your own excuses.

Before moving on, we need to address a very important aspect of accountability: You can't hold someone accountable if you're not practicing what you're preaching. This is why a Heartbeat must be highly accountable, and the Allies. They will make the situation worse if they call someone out for something they're terrible at. You can't be a 50 percent attender scolding a 30 percent attender. Accountability must come from integrity.

Coaches, this is why you need to show up to workouts and shootarounds. There's no point in telling your players to attend something you aren't willing to attend yourself. You can't have your assistant coaches running the summer league while you're on the beach texting your players that they need to show up. Make sure your coaches and leaders all understand this. Accountability done wrong burns bridges.

The process of accountability is built on repetition and habits. Some days, you'll have to motivate yourself more than others. You'll be tempted to take shortcuts or overlook small things, but it's those small things that shape your culture over time. Every interaction, every correction, and every moment of encouragement adds up.

Take note of the five steps in the accountability loop. I've included a practical example in my outline.

1. CLEAR STANDARD

Team rule: Everyone needs to show up ready for practice by the exact time practice begins.

2. IMMEDIATE RECOGNITION OF DEVIATION

Timmy has shown up three to five minutes late several times this week.

3. PRIVATE CORRECTION

Rather than turning a blind eye, because it seems like a rather minor issue to fuss over, you tell Timmy you'd like to talk to him after practice. When you talk, you choose *grace* or *truth*. Grace would include a gentle nudging and a loving comment. Truth would include telling him that his actions are unacceptable and irresponsible.

4. OPPORTUNITY FOR REDEMPTION

You end by saying you'll give him one more chance. If he can make it on time from here on out, we'll move on. If not, there will be consequences. You make sure to inform parents if you feel it's appropriate.

5. FOLLOW-UP

You check in with Timmy the next few days and ask if he's had any issues in getting there on time. If he fixes the behavior, you tell him that you're proud of him.

Building accountability is a lot like creating a masterpiece. Picture a sculptor standing before a massive block of marble. As yet, it has no form or beauty, but the artist can visualize what it will become. With each careful strike of the chisel, the vision starts to take shape. It takes thousands of small, deliberate hits before the statue finally reveals itself.

The sculptor must trust the process. He has to believe in what he's creating long before anyone else can see it. He must be patient, consistent, and intentional with every swing of the hammer. One rushed or careless strike could undo hours of progress.

Coach, your team is your sculpture. You have to see the finished product in your mind before the season begins. Handle your team with care and stay consistent—especially when you're not seeing results. Some days will be harder than others, but don't stop chiseling. Over time, those small, faithful efforts will reveal something beautiful: a team shaped by accountability, trust, and purpose.

APPLICATION

1. How do you currently hold your players and coaches accountable? Are you consistent in your expectations?
2. How many times throughout the season do you revisit your goals, standards, and expectations?
3. In what areas might you be asking players to do something you aren't fully modeling yourself? How can you improve your integrity in those areas?
4. Is your Heartbeat player keeping his or her teammates accountable? How?
5. How do you prioritize winning games versus maintaining team standards and accountability?

6. Do I naturally lean toward excessive grace or excessive truth? How does that impact my team?
7. How do I respond (verbally and nonverbally) when players fail?
8. Are there players in your program that need to be held accountable now although it's scary what the fallout could do to your success?
9. What are your strengths in the area of accountability? Make a list.
10. What are your weaknesses in the area of accountability? Make a list.

CHAPTER 12

SHARED RECOGNITION

THE ROOT OF much contempt in a locker room stems from bitterness or jealousy. Unfortunately, it's a huge part of our society at large.

"I'm better than him, and he gets to play."

"How come she gets all the credit?"

Once you start playing the comparison game, you begin building a grudge mountain. Life will never be fair. Parents would often tell me it wasn't fair that other kids were playing over their child. I'd respond, "Fair? If I played your kid, that would *not* be fair. Your son has come to 15 percent of our workouts and barely pushes himself in practice. The kid playing over him spent the entire summer in a gym rather than swimming or running around like your son did."

Fair is getting what you've earned. First and foremost, let's establish that life is not about everything being equally distributed. You earn what you deserve. It's important that your team understands this. Equality and equity are often confused: Equality is getting the same; equity is getting what you deserve or need. When a parent makes claims about equality, it's important to stress that equality isn't your concern—equity is.

Regardless of the occasional complaining parent, your job as a coach is to keep your team together. It's a never-ending balancing act. But here's some good news: You *can* make your life easier. There are ways to set yourself up for cultural success before the problems rise to the surface. You won't have to constantly remedy disgruntled athletes if they feel included and appreciated. Let's look at several ways to build a sense of community in your program, starting with making even bench players feel like an important part of the team.

RECOGNIZE CONTRIBUTIONS

Point out what bench players do well. Whether in practice or in games, these athletes rarely receive recognition. They're expected to put in massive effort while receiving no reward. They'll never have the highlight of the night. They may not get reps in game-plan drills. Like Nike, we expect them to "just do it."

Here's your solution: Tell them, "Good job." I know, it seems simple, almost too simple. But a sincere "good job" goes a long way. Something that takes you almost no effort can dramatically improve team culture. How often do you acknowledge your scout team for practicing hard? Every day, I hope.

One of my favorite strategies was making film cuts of bench players celebrating during games. Think about it: They watch from the sidelines, then the next day watch the same game again while hearing about their teammates' great plays. They've now spent four hours watching a game that they didn't participate in. If you think that's fun for them, you're wrong. The first time I showed the bench reaction highlights, I saw undeniable pride in their eyes. Their contribution was being acknowledged. If you ask them for energy during games, you should reward it, highlight it. Find unique ways to make every player feel that they've contributed to the team's success.

After my first season coaching varsity, I realized I needed to find creative ways to recognize the plays that don't show up in the box score. In basketball, that means effort plays, such as diving for loose balls, sprinting back on defense, taking a charge, or fighting for a rebound. Those are the kinds of plays that change games, but they rarely get the spotlight. That's when the idea for The Wall of Hustle was born.

> Reward the effort that wins games, not just the stats that make headlines.

I set aside a section of our locker room wall to honor those effort plays. Anytime a player made a hustle play, I'd go back through the game film, screenshot the moment, and print it out. On each photo, I wrote the player's name, the game, and a short note about what they did—then taped it up on the wall. As the season progressed, the wall started filling with pictures. Before long, it became something special.

The Wall of Hustle gave recognition to the gritty, tough players who usually worked in the shadows. The scorers still got their headlines, but now the grinders got their moment too. It quickly became a source of pride for the team. When a player's picture went up, he'd light up with a huge smile. It even pushed the quieter or less aggressive players to get tougher, because they wanted to earn a spot on that wall.

Over the next five years, our teams built a reputation for it. We took more charges than any team we played. Opponents couldn't get to the rim without running into a body. Hustle, grit, and toughness became our calling card—and it all started with one wall and a simple idea: reward the effort that wins games, not just the stats that make headlines.

ATTRIBUTE SUCCESS TO EVERYONE

Use "we" in interviews, social media, and classroom conversations. Avoid putting yourself or your best player on a pedestal. Kids notice when a "favorite" appears, whether it's intentional or not. Eventually, players who never receive recognition will stop trying, because they feel you don't care.

ASK FOR THE OPINIONS OF EVERYONE

Items like warm-up shirt design, pregame music, or drill preferences are often only assigned to the best players. We default to asking those who produce the most stats, assuming it's part of a captain's duty. For decisions that don't directly affect performance, like shirt color, ask everyone. It's easy and shows that every voice matters.

PAY ATTENTION TO EVERYONE

In 2020, Pete Carroll and Steve Kerr produced a podcast together entitled *Flying Coach* to share coaching stories and advice. One anecdote stood out: Steve Kerr asked how Carroll built the Seattle Seahawks culture from historic afterthought to Super

Bowl winners. Carroll's first point? Before every practice, during warm-ups, he talked to the guys in the back of the line.

It sounds minor, but it's huge. In most sports, before practice officially starts, teams do a stretch routine. In football, players are aligned by importance: captains up front, starters in the middle, bench players in the back. The captains and starters already want to be there; they have incentive to perform and protect their roles. The bench? They're about to endure a long, grueling practice and are expected to push others while often unseen. Coaches usually stay up front with the stars, laughing and humanizing themselves. Rarely do they interact with the back-of-the-line players.

Carroll's advice is brilliant. Paying attention to role players during warm-ups can completely improve effort and attitude in practice. Every human wants to be seen. Feeling seen instantly improves attitude and work ethic.

If you want an elite culture, it requires you to care about every player. Every single player gets your love. Every single manager gets your time. Every single coach gets a voice.

APPLICATION

1. Write a thank-you note to the coaches on your staff. It can be simple or elaborate. Show them that you value their contribution to the program.
2. Think about whether you might be sending verbal or non-verbal messages that could be creating jealousy among the players or coaches.
3. Think of one way that you can recognize the non-statistical efforts of your players.

4. Plan how to spend equal amounts of time getting to know *all* players. How could you spend more time with the fringe players?
5. Ensure that your team social media accounts give credit to all players at some point during the season.
6. Be intentional, and encourage your staff to be intentional, about saying simple phrases—"good job," "thank you," "great energy"—often.
7. List your strengths in the area of sharing recognition.
8. List your weaknesses in the area of sharing recognition.

CHAPTER 13

VOICES

PERHAPS THE MOST important factor in determining your team culture is your voice. You may have heard the old saying, "Sticks and stones may break my bones, but words will never hurt me." I don't know about you, but I've been hurt by words. I think I've been crushed by words more often than by physical ailments, especially in a school full of kids who can't fully control what they say. I used to hear wildly offensive things from my students and even their parents. I'd drive home upset and angry on occasion. So let's start here: Words matter. They hurt. They heal. They divide. They unite.

The value of words cannot be underestimated.

- Wars are started with a voice: *"I declare war."*
- Marriages are certified with a voice: *"I do."*
- Friendships are made with a voice: *"Do you want to hang out?"*
- Arrests are made with a voice: *"You are under arrest."*

YOUR VOICE IS USED IN MANY WAYS IN SPORTS.

FEEDBACK

Feedback can flow in any direction: coach-to-coach, coach-to-player, or player-to-player. We often think of feedback as a coach correcting a player's mistake, but it's much more than that.

Feedback can be discussing a JV game with your staff to help them improve or listening to an assistant coach's ideas about your scheme. Players are constantly giving each other feedback, whether positive or negative: *You got this. Head up, next play. You're killing us! Dude, pass the ball!*

Teams that normalize feedback show the most growth during the season. Most people are comfortable giving feedback, but few desire to be on the receiving end. Later in the chapter, you'll read about helpful strategies to create a culture of healthy feedback interactions.

PERSONAL INTERACTIONS

These are your day-to-day conversations at school, at church, or in the community. Your interactions matter more than you realize. This is where the most bridges are burned. Coaches sometimes forget who they are outside a team-sanctioned event. They might get drunk or dip their toe in gossip. The best practice is to remain professional at all times when working with kids. People will find ways to be offended at anything and everything, so be on your guard. Aim to always be positive. Keep team business in-house. I stressed this to my assistants every year: if it's about the team, discuss it with staff only. If someone wants to talk about a game, keep it vague and positive.

Most situations in which a coach feels burned by someone and loses trust arise from a breach of trust in a personal interaction. The coaches in my leadership cohort expressed that, early in their careers, they were all hurt because they shared something personal with a parent and it came back to bite them. It's true of any relationship in life: You can't hide from people forever, but you also can't be loose-lipped. I think the best rule of thumb is to avoid gossip in general. If you want to talk about a player or parent, keep it within the staff. The rewards do not even come close to the risks.

During my first year as freshman team basketball coach, when I was ripe out of college, my wife and I were supported and embraced by some amazing families. We felt like a close family and had an amazing season. The next year, I was promoted to JV so had the rare opportunity to coach the same group two years in a row. Some good players didn't improve at all and became average players. Some average players became good players. When the first game tipped off, a few parents were in complete shock that their son, who had been a good freshman athlete, was now coming off the bench. Our family feelings quickly evaporated. Some parents who had embraced my wife soon gave her the cold shoulder.

I was immediately grateful that I had declined attending their post-game bar visits and drinking parties. They had invited my wife and I to all their get-togethers. It was easy for me to see the big picture and how that was a bad idea, so I always respectfully declined. Little did I know that I had been protecting myself from what was to come. If I had joined their parties, I would more than likely have over-shared information and made myself an easy target. So in JV, even though they decided they only wanted to support me if their son was playing, I knew they couldn't do anything to hurt me.

CONVERTING EMOTIONS

Your voice is your emotional outlet. How often have you apologized to a friend or family member for saying something offensive during an emotional outburst? Coaches are no different. Screaming at kids during games isn't always about malice; it's often anger, embarrassment, or frustration. The key is control.

We're human, and we'll get angry. It's the adult's responsibility to manage emotions.

Many veteran coaches tell me they were hotheads when they were younger. They overreacted and let every loss feel like a personal indictment. Young coaches need experienced mentors on staff to help them overcome the *pride* that's hard to shake in the beginning. Veteran coaches bring life experience and wisdom. You must release the thought that the world is scrutinizing your record after every game. The truth is that no one will remember twenty-four hours from now. Adults have their own problems. They won't be focused on yours.

Your goal is for your team and staff to respect you, not fear you. In the heat of the moment, those two can feel similar, and coaches often confuse them. Fear is a quick fix, an immediate way to gain compliance, but respect is a long-term solution.

When people obey out of fear, they operate with reduced potential. Their focus shifts to avoiding mistakes rather than making an impact. But when they follow out of respect, they still obey—only now they feel supported, trusted, and free to take meaningful risks.

These two approaches get muddled, because both result in obedience. But, coaches, obedience alone does not build a strong culture. Fearful obedience lowers your ceiling. Respectful obedience raises it—and leads to high-impact performance.

We've established that voices are crucial to success in sports, so let's talk about how to use them effectively. Your voice can either build your culture or break it down, depending on how you use it. The best coaches and leaders understand that good communication includes *how*, *when*, and *why* you speak, not just *what* you say. You can use your voice in several ways to shape a top-tier team culture, and mastering this skill can completely transform the way your team connects and competes.

CALL UP, NOT OUT

In the heat of competition, it's natural to want to yell at someone who made a mental error. Players and coaches do it repeatedly. Coaches have more leeway, but frequent yelling creates fear rather than improvement, and fear leads to timidity. You'll get 75 percent of a player's potential, at most, if they're afraid.

With young athletes, default to *calling up*, not *calling out*. Calling out makes someone feel bad for a mistake; calling up identifies the mistake, provides a solution, and instills hope.

Calling out: "How can you run the wrong route? We've practiced this a hundred times. That's terrible, kid!"

Calling up: "Hey, man, you ran your route at five yards, but we wanted ten. We have to get it right, but I know you can. Let's lock in."

Which would you prefer? It's obvious that 100 percent of athletes will respond better to being called up. Deep down we all know this. I believe the true motivation in calling someone out is pride. It's a coach being embarrassed that his or her team isn't performing well. We've all been there, self-conscious about what people might think about us. If we can make it look like it's the players' fault, the fans might not see that it's our coaching that needs work, not the players.

One of the worst things a coach can yell during a game is "We practiced this!" You might as well be yelling to the entire bleachers that it's the kid's fault, not yours. Pride ruins relationships. Don't let it happen.

MAKE IT CLEAR THAT THE PLAYERS ARE NOT THE COACHES

One of my pet peeves was when one of my players would yell at another player. This goes hand in hand with the previous section. Players get too comfortable calling each other out. For my teams, I had a simple rule: Players play. Coaches coach. I didn't want anyone wearing a uniform to think they had authority over others. I'd often break it down this way conversationally:

Coach: "How many of you have ever made a mistake and played better after a teammate yelled at you?"

No hands raised.

Coach: "How many of you ever needed a teammate yelling at you to realize that you made a mistake?"

No hands raised.

Coach: "How many of you actually play worse after getting yelled at?"

Hands raised.

Coach: "So why are we yelling at each other? You've all just admitted that it doesn't help you mentally or physically. So why are we so comfortable hurting our own team? Can we at least let the other team beat us rather than beating ourselves?"

You need to explain things with complete clarity. Always err on the side of over-explaining team culture expectations.

BE CURIOUS

Curiosity is one of the most powerful tools in a coach's toolbox. Far beyond teaching skills or running drills, it involves understanding your players as people. Every athlete has a story. Their past experiences, family life, friendships, challenges, and interests all shape who they are on and off the court. If you approach players with curiosity rather than judgment, you unlock a deeper level of trust and engagement.

Think of it like this: When a player misbehaves or underperforms, it's easy to react with frustration. *Why aren't they trying?* or *They don't care about the team!* are common responses. But a curious coach asks questions instead: *What's going on outside of practice? Is something bothering you? What can I do to help you improve?* These questions show players that you care about them as individuals, not just as athletes.

A famous scene in *Ted Lasso* illustrates this perfectly. Ted, an American football coach with almost no experience in European soccer, takes over a failing Premier League team. Most people expect him to be a joke. In one viral moment, Ted ends up in a pub playing darts against a local bully who assumes he's clueless. The bully trash-talks, makes fun of him, and confidently wagers a high-stakes bet, certain Ted can't compete. But Ted casually asks if he can play left-handed, and from that moment, the tone shifts. He starts sinking bull's-eyes with ease. The bully's face falls as Ted not only wins but dominates.

Before throwing the final dart, Ted delivers a line that has become iconic: "People make assumptions because they're not curious." If the bully had bothered to ask a single question about Ted's background instead of judging him, he might have learned that Ted grew up playing darts with his father every Sunday. All those years of practice shaped the very skill the bully underestimated. A simple act of curiosity—one honest question—could have changed the outcome entirely.

Coaches fall into this the same trap when they make assumptions about their players instead of being curious. You might think you know why a kid is acting out, shutting down, or slacking off, but unless you ask, you're only guessing. Curiosity uncovers the real story. Maybe the player who looks lazy is actually overwhelmed. Maybe the one with a bad attitude is dealing with something at home. Maybe the quiet kid who never speaks is desperate for connection but doesn't know how to initiate it. When coaches choose curiosity over assumptions, they unlock doors that judgments keep shut.

Being curious means understanding the person behind the behavior so you can coach them more effectively. Curiosity gives you access to hearts you might otherwise never reach.

If you take the time to understand your athletes' motivations, struggles, and perspectives, you can make better decisions about how to communicate, train, and lead them. Curiosity allows you to:

- *Build trust.* Players feel valued when you genuinely want to know who they are.
- *Improve performance.* Understanding what drives a player can help you tailor instruction to their strengths and weaknesses.
- *Prevent conflicts.* Many behavior issues stem from misunderstandings. Curiosity helps you uncover the root causes before they escalate.

When you seek to understand the person, you find solutions more quickly. You might find out the player showing up late every day takes care of his or her younger siblings because the parents are absent. Or that the kid who can't make a free throw is struggling to focus because dad has been laid off from his job and they don't know whether they'll have to move or not.

Not every bad habit has a hidden cause, but many do. And if there *is* a deeper reason behind a player's behavior, the last thing you want is to make it worse by failing to ask the right questions.

Your words are both your fatal flaw and your secret weapon. Controlling your voice with your staff and players gives your team culture a fighting chance at greatness.

APPLICATION

1. Do your players fear or respect you? If you don't know, ask the coaches on your staff. Why did you answer the way you did?
2. Would the tone of your voice match the culture you claim to value if someone recorded your practices?
3. Do you personally interact with every player and coach in your program?
4. Does your coaching staff get intentional feedback on their performance and contribution?
5. How often do you receive feedback from other coaches?
6. Ask your Heartbeat, "Does the team think I call them out or call them up?"
7. Ask your coaching staff, "Do you feel like you have a voice in this program?"
8. What situations consistently trigger your emotional overreactions?

9. What are your strengths in the area of communication?
10. What are your weaknesses in the area of communication?

CHAPTER 14

PRIDE

THE ULTIMATE DESTROYER of relationships is pride. Whether it's a coach-player relationship or any other kind, the fastest way to break it apart is to allow pride to govern your actions. Pride leads to jealousy, shortcuts, anger, bitterness, and avoidance. If your relationship was a movie, pride would be the big bad villain.

Pride is blinding. It prevents you from seeing oncoming conflict, and when you're in the conflict it keeps you from being able to own your part in it. It convinces you that accountability is for everyone else. It whispers that you're always right, that your way is the only way, and that compromise is weakness. Pride distorts your view of others and of yourself.

But if pride is the villain, humility is the hero. Humility is the strength to recognize that you're not the center of the universe and that you don't need to be. It's the willingness to listen, to learn, and to admit when you've fallen short. Humility keeps you from placing yourself at the top of the priority list and gives you the clarity to see what the team really needs.

Pride is blinding. It prevents you from seeing oncoming conflict, and when you're in the conflict it keeps you from being able to own your part in it.

When a leader chooses humility, walls drop fast. People stop feeling threatened. Communication opens up. Players become more willing to buy into a message, because they trust the messenger. When you move from pride to humility, your team will very quickly buy into whatever message you want to sell them—and not because they have to but because they want to.

In my first three seasons of being a head coach, I didn't seek out an assistant. I didn't post a job for it. I didn't ask anyone. At the time, I attributed my reasoning to frugality. After all, it was a small school and a program without funding. We couldn't afford the luxury of having "extra help." But if you gave me truth serum, I would tell you it was pride. I didn't want accountability. I didn't want to the pressure of communicating all my thoughts with one more person. I didn't want to be tied to another person. I wanted to do it myself and live in my own echo chamber, without anyone to question my process, call me up to better behavior, or suggest we try something else.

In year four, I met a guy at my church who was a JV coach in the community. My family and his got together for dinner one night in the summer. During dinner, I muttered, "You should join my staff. It'd be fun." Truthfully, it was just something I said. I didn't think about whether I meant it or not. I thought it was a drive-by comment you just say out of flattery, but a few days later, he gave me a call. After I answered, he didn't skip a beat: "Hey man, I thought about your offer. I'll do it." I immediately had to reorient myself and think about what my offer was. Panicking, I said, "Awesome! We'll be in touch."

Later, I looked back on this as an act of God. I fell face-first into a blessing that I didn't know I needed. I never said a word to him about the fact that I hadn't meant the offer. Andrew, if you're reading this, I'm sorry, and I'm thrilled that I put my foot in my mouth.

When the season came, I had to adjust to having a second person to explain everything to. The first few days, I forgot to make copies of my practice plan. As the days, weeks, and months went by, I realized that I'd been a fool for the previous three years. Having an assistant coach was amazing. He talked me off ledges when I was struggling. He gave me excellent ideas about how to game-plan. His presence balanced mine with the boys. And the ultimate perk—he became one of my best friends.

Pride had blinded me to a problem that was painfully obvious. It was a semi-truck barreling straight toward me, and I refused to acknowledge it. I was so afraid of being questioned, so desperate to appear in control, that I ended up hurting my entire program. That's the thing about pride: in the moment, it feels complicated. It feels justified. It feels like protecting yourself. But when you look back, it's embarrassingly clear.

> When you're the head decision-maker, you drag the whole team into your blind spots. Your pride and your ego become their obstacle.

The signs were there. The warnings were loud. I just didn't want to see them.

When you're the head decision-maker, you drag the whole team into your blind spots. Your pride and your ego become their obstacle. Your fear becomes their ceiling. Pride at the top can quietly corrupt everything beneath it, and the worst part is that you won't realize the damage until long after it's been done.

Pride can take over a coach in many ways:

- Not respecting the referees—because you can see the violations better than they can
- Not giving your assistant coaches a voice—because they'd only slow you down
- Not allowing the players to have input in the game plan—because they're nowhere near as smart as you
- Not moving on from a schematic decision that isn't working—because it's actually the players fault and not yours

These attitudes can corrupt a program and assuredly create a lack of care in your team.

What happens if your players are struggling with pride? More than likely, they belong in the Vortex category. They display actions such as shaking their head when being coached, arguing with officials, showing poor sportsmanship, not following their team leaders, and questioning the coach's decisions. When pride enters the equation, remember, the first step is creating an awareness of the problem.

A major danger with pride is that it's contagious. Pride in a leader gives permission for pride in players. Pride creates "micro-cults" on a team, little groups that think they know better. Pride fractures roles: seniors vs. underclassmen, starters vs. bench, leaders vs. followers. Pride makes communication horizontal (player-to-player complaining) instead of vertical (player-to-coach problem-solving). Pride can quickly escalate from an individual problem to an organization problem.

Here's a humility action list for you to consider. If you want to develop muscle memory that defaults your mindset to humility rather than pride, consider these things.

INVITE ASSISTANTS TO CHALLENGE GAME PLANS

It's easy for a head coach to want to prove himself by planning out everything independently. They're thinking, *No one can question who is responsible for the success if I can just do it all myself* or *No one else on my staff is as smart as I am, so I'm going to do it all alone to avoid a time-consuming conversation.*

There are several issues with that kind of thinking. You won't be prepared to deviate. If there's no "what-if" discussed, you probably won't be ready for your ideas to be countered during the competition. Your coaching staff will start to disengage or even resent you. They're thinking, *Why should I even try if I'm not being involved?* which will get more intense as the season progresses. Lastly, you're not preparing your staff for their future. They need to learn from you. You can't be fully prepared solely by watching. Part of your job as a head coach is to prepare your staff for their goals.

When I coached JV basketball, my boss did everything he could to help me get a varsity job. He explained the *why* of everything he did. He delegated tasks to me that he knew would stretch me. When I struggled, he made sure to push me through. When I was thriving, he brought me back down to earth. He constantly sought to prepare me to become a successful head coach.

Some coaches don't do that. Their prideful mindset tells them that if something doesn't directly connect to winning, it's not worth it. I've heard stories of varsity coaches not saying a word to their JV coaches for an entire season. To them, the varsity assistant coaches were the only ones worth bouncing ideas off. As a head coach, you're an investor. You're not only investing in your players but your staff also. I can tell you from experience that when my head coach went above and beyond for me, it made me go above and beyond for him. I was eager to go the extra mile, because I cared about the captain of the ship and didn't want to let him down.

ASK PLAYERS, "WHAT ARE YOU SEEING OUT THERE?"

Every single halftime of every single game I coached I asked my players one question: *What are you seeing out there?* I asked because their thoughts were extremely important to me. Not only because they were closer to the action than I was, but because it gave them ownership in the process. I didn't give them the steering wheel, but I let them sit in the front seat with me. Occasionally I'd even try out an idea of theirs that I knew was safe to try. I wanted them to know I wasn't patronizing them; I wanted them to be invested in the process.

When you give people ownership they care more about the process. Think about your own place of work. Coaches of youth or school sports usually have a separate full-time job. In that job, would you feel like investing in the process if your boss never asked you what your thoughts were? No way. If your boss met with you before or after big meetings and asked for your thoughts, you'd feel like an important part of the process. You'd feel included. It's the same for your players; they're human just like us. They don't feel less emotion than you because they're younger.

Inviting my players into the conversation was both a strategy and a statement. It told them that I didn't need to have all the answers. That simple posture shattered any illusion of hierarchy that pride tries to create. When a leader is willing to hear from the people he leads, the room shifts. Trust grows. Walls fall. Players stop performing *for* you and start performing *with* you.

And best of all, when players feel heard, they become more honest. They'll tell you what's really happening instead of what they think you want to hear. Pride demands control, but humility invites contribution, and contribution is where buy-in begins.

ACKNOWLEDGE YOUR MISTAKES OPENLY AFTER A LOSS

When a team loses, people look for someone to blame. Only in the healthiest teams do they all mutually take accountability. In an unhealthy state of mind entrenched in pride, coaches, athletes, administrators, and even parents, all blame each other. I'd hear it frequently from a wide variety of people. Parents blamed the coaches. Coaches said the team didn't execute their perfect game plan. Players pointed the finger at each other. In a toxic culture, blame is the antecedent of every loss.

It's a powerful statement, as a coach, to take the blame whether you think you deserve it or not. You are sending a message louder than any pregame speech you'll ever give. You're demonstrating ultimate humility. Pride says, "Not my fault." Humility says, "Whether it's my fault or not, I'll carry it." Your team will take notice. You're not only removing a target from the locker room, you're also eliminating the instinct to blame. And when players see a leader willingly shoulder responsibility, it becomes almost impossible for them to hide behind excuses. You're modeling humility in real time, and modeling is far more powerful than lecturing.

When you consistently take ownership, something subtle but transformational happens: Your players start doing the same. Suddenly, the point guard admits he missed a rotation. The senior acknowledges he took a bad shot. The bench guy says he didn't bring enough energy. Accountability becomes contagious. Humility spreads. The culture shifts from *Who messed up?* to *How do we fix it together?* It all starts when the person with the most authority chooses to lead with the least ego.

Pride is the silent killer of teams, cultures, and relationships, but humility is the force that brings them back to life. Pride isolates; humility connects. Pride hardens; humility softens. Pride blinds; humility illuminates. A leader who chooses humility is changing the entire environment: communication becomes honest, roles become clearer, trust becomes stronger, and accountability becomes shared.

The health of your program will always reflect the posture of your heart. If you lead with pride, your team will fracture. But if you lead with humility—inviting input, owning mistakes, elevating others—your team will not only follow you; they'll fight for you. In the long run, humility will make you a better coach and a better person. It will also make your team a better family.

APPLICATION

1. Do you give assistant coaches and players the ability to have an appropriate amount of input in your decision-making? If not, where are some areas that you can let them in?
2. How much do you allow the players to speak on their performance in a competition vs. you speaking the entire time?
3. What are the current "micro-cults" in your program—groups with their own agenda or hierarchy? How can you encourage them to bring down their walls and be a part of the one team?
4. What's one pride-driven habit you will intentionally eliminate this season?
5. How much do you delegate to those who work with or for you? Rate yourself on a scale of 1 to 10 (most = 10). How can you improve that rating?
6. How comfortable are you with not having your own voice heard if you're an assistant and not a decision-maker? Rate yourself on a scale of 1 to 10 (10 = most comfortable).

CHAPTER 15

TIMES ARE CHANGIN'

I N 1964 BOB Dylan released his iconic song "The Times They Are A-Changin'," a poetic call for awareness and adaptation as the world around him shifted in ways that could no longer be ignored.

Over half a century later, his words still ring true, especially in the world of sports. The culture of athletes has changed dramatically over time. Today's players are shaped by a different world—one filled with technology, instant gratification, social media platforms, being overly stimulated, and new expectations of leadership and belonging. Coaches who once relied on authority and repetition now find themselves needing connection and communication. To be effective in this new era, coaches must not resist change but learn to evolve with it, because, as Dylan warned, "You better start swimmin', or you'll sink like a stone."

The current generation has deviated from the norms of previous generations in many ways. Behaviorally, concepts like accountability, patience, and coachability are seemingly becoming more elusive. Parents are becoming more overwhelming by the year.

A large portion of administrators have started prohibiting tough love in the name of sensitivity. Not too long ago, people in the business world received their performance reviews quarterly. Athletes received theirs at the end of each season. Now? People need immediate feedback. Anxious minds need to be calmed continuously. Parents want to know why their child isn't happy as soon as possible. Players demand to know why they aren't playing as much as others on a weekly basis.

However, these kinds of changes aren't a new phenomenon. The truth is, *every generation believes the one after them has it easier, but that doesn't change our responsibility to reach those we lead.* Complaining doesn't connect. Coaches have to find ways to healthily adapt.

> Adapting calls for maintaining your standards while finding new ways to uphold them in a changing world.

How do you decide how you're going to adapt? Skeptics would say: stand on principle, be rigid, and refuse to cave in. They might believe that compromise is never an option. Unfortunately, those coaches will soon find themselves in the midst of a tumultuous locker room culture. Let's face it: Change is hard. We don't seek out change because it's fun. We do it because it's necessary.

The other side of that double-edged sword is becoming too compromising. If you bend too far to please everyone, you risk losing the very standards that make your program strong. The challenge is to find balance and adapt without abandoning your core values. Great coaches know how to evolve their methods while keeping their message the same. They hold players accountable, but with empathy. They maintain high expectations, but with understanding. Adapting calls for maintaining your standards while finding new ways to uphold them in a changing world.

I always considered myself as someone who held tightly to the reins. Delegation wasn't my friend. My preferred methods were the only ways things should be done. Period. Whether it was me or someone else carrying them out didn't matter. When I started coaching, I entered the position with a firm belief that uniformity in appearance was a necessity for a team. Our colors were red and white, and I wanted everything to match. Shoes? Red and white. Socks? Red or white. Warm-up shirts? You guessed it, red and white.

But a major change in the younger generation is the development of individuality. Kids want to stand out more. They want to be unique. They don't want to fit into a mold. My color preferences were met with sighs and eye rolls. One year, after carefully listening to my Heartbeat, I decided to compromise. I let them buy whatever shoes they wanted. I even allowed black warm-up shirts. I still held firm standards for how we represented ourselves—but I found a way to meet them where they were.

The result was eye-opening. They were happier. We argued less about things that didn't matter. Most importantly, I showed them that I heard them and that I was trying to understand them. It cost me nothing. It would've been a nonsensical hill to die on. As a coach, you have to learn when to stand firm and

> The art of adaptation lies in knowing which hills are worth defending and which are simply blocking your view of the bigger picture.

when to step aside. The art of adaptation lies in knowing which hills are worth defending and which are simply blocking your view of the bigger picture.

In the Netflix documentary *Court of Gold*, which follows the 2024 Summer Olympic basketball teams, Serbian head coach Svetislav Pešić features heavily. With a coaching career dating back to 1982, Pešić offers thoughtful insight into how the mentality of athletes has changed over time. When asked about modern players, he notes, "Most coaches, we think we can control everything. It's not like that. Today's players also watch you, analyze you, to see when they can slip away or gain something. . . . Nowadays, the job of a coach is more complicated than it was back in my day."[5]

He's right. Today's younger generation questions everything. Earlier generations simply did what they were told; now, players want to know *why*. They evaluate you as much as you evaluate them. They want the reasoning behind the instruction, not just the instruction itself. Trust is no longer linear. It's more like a web.

So what do you do with that shift? Fight it? I hope not. Fighting cultural change only leads to frustration and bitterness. Learning how to adjust, on the other hand, extends your career and builds trust with your players. Pešić goes on to add, "A coach must never put himself ahead of the team."[6] That includes preferences. Don't compromise your non-negotiables but learn to adapt in the areas that aren't worth the battle.

Regardless of how the times change, always *be you*. An adaptation should never include your personality. The human body has an unidentifiable gene that allows us to sniff out inauthenticity. When you start with a new team or have a new group come in, you'll feel an urge to try to be a coach that you're not. Maybe it's acting more serious. Or trying to sound cooler. It could be several things. The funny thing about kids, as absent-minded as they appear to be, is that they catch on to social cues very quickly. One of the fastest ways to lose your team is for them to think you're a phony.

To test this theory out at a much higher competitive level, I contacted my friend Luke St. Lifer, the director of basketball operations for Virginia Commonwealth University (VCU). I asked him, "How much should a coach change who he or she is in an effort to reach the hearts of their team?"

He responded, "At the end of the day, as coaches, we have to look in the mirror and ask ourselves what our intent is? The players we coach are brilliant, extremely observant people. If they know how much you care about them, you can coach them harder than ever. Because they know your intent. They know your care factor. If the foundation of your program is built on trust, care factor, and loyalty, the winds of NIL and transfer portal can blow any which way. Your house will stay strong.

"I believe the word *enhance* is more suitable. Enhance your relationships, enhance your intent, enhance your purpose. Enhancing isn't changing, it's seeing more clearly your purpose and your why. Which ultimately has the ability to translate to whatever version of college athletics is to come, past, present, and future. Authenticity is everything, and it will get you burnt sometimes. But there's no better top recruit, game-winning shot, or championship won than knowing you did things the right way with the right intentions regardless of the environment around you."

Luke is right, you have to be authentic. It's important to grasp that you can wisely adjust to the cultural trends without selling out on who you are. It's a very hard line to toe, but if you're intentional about it, it can be done.

To better understand how coaches are adjusting to the changing times, I asked three highly successful high school coaches for their wisdom. I selected individuals from different sports, both men and women, so their insight would reflect a broad, well-rounded range of experiences and posed the following question.

Q: The future of coaching will look different than it does right now. Up until the 2000s, coaches didn't have to connect with athletes as much. They could be way more aggressive in their delivery. How do you adjust as culture adjusts? Do you think we'll go through another culture shift in your career?

JOSHUA O'CONNOR

Head football and track and field coach for Sun Prairie West High School in Sun Prairie, Wisconsin.

ANSWER

"Coaching, to me, has and always will be focused on building a relationship founded on trust. As our culture changes, so too does the way we build trust. In the past, it was much easier for an individual in a position of power to be trusted simply because of their title. The "old-school approach" to coaching that was more aggressive could happen because being a coach was a title of respect, and athletes trusted their coach because that's what they were supposed to do. Now, it takes more time and work to build trust with athletes, because we encourage individuals in our society to question and seek understanding. With how technology is pushing changes in our society, I'm sure there will be culture shifts that coaches my age will have to adjust to, though I'm not sure what that change will be. Many people say the pendulum will swing back the other way, but I'm not sure if that will be the case."

MALLORY LIEBL

Assistant girls' basketball coach for Milliken University.

ANSWER

"I agree that the culture has changed, but I believe that building relationships has always been and will always be most important. Building relationships can be very challenging at times—sometimes personalities don't mesh well—but if you truly take the time to care about all players off the court and build that trust with them, not only can you coach kids with intensity, but you can also be a great resource for them off the court. Just because someone has "coach" before their name, doesn't make it ok to berate and disrespect them. I believe that also goes for coaches to players; being a coach doesn't give you the right to completely tear a kid down.

"What I cherish most as a coach is watching kids grow as players and people, during their time in our program and as they move on in life, continuing to be involved in their lives in a different capacity. I believe as long as that relationship piece is kept at the forefront, the changing culture won't mean changing your coaching style. I think the culture will continue to shift, it's shifted so much just in my coaching career to this point, and it seems like every year brings new ways of coaching, new ideas, and new concepts."

JAY BENISH

Head boys' basketball coach at Oconomowoc High School in Oconomowoc, Wisconsin.

Jay is also on the board for the Wisconsin Basketball Coaches Association, where he runs the state coaching clinic.

ANSWER

"I honestly look at coaching as not necessarily having to make these shifts with culture but more as knowing your players, who they are, and what they need to be successful on and off the floor. That way, you can continue to grow the culture in a way that gets their buy-in without sacrificing the foundation and expectations that are set in your culture. I think you can coach forever and have success as long as you are willing to continue to grow along with the game and stay connected to what is relevant in the times. Things are constantly changing and becoming better or worse, but if you have strong values that you live by and hold people accountable to, then the rest of the changes are really trends and ideas that you either grow with or lose sight of."

The common theme among these three stalwart coaches is that no matter how the culture changes, you must find ways to connect heart to heart. That's the theme of this entire book: *How does a coach today connect with every heart in the locker room?* As culture shifts, the methods of connection shift with it. You don't need to change who you are, nor should you. But you *do* need a pulse on your team, an awareness of how to adapt in healthy, meaningful ways. That adaptability is what allows you to build the strongest possible culture for team success.

APPLICATION

1. What is the hardest cultural movement with athletes that you've struggled to embrace?
2. What is one stance you've taken that you will not change regardless of the changing times?
3. What is one area in which you could adapt your approach this season without sacrificing the heart of your standards?
4. How well do you think you've done at trying to understand the next generation vs. judging them? Rate yourself on a scale of 1 to 10 (10 = most judgmental)
5. Can you think of a time when you were a young athlete when a coach went above and beyond to try to understand you? What did that do for you?
6. What are appropriate freedoms that you can give your team in the age of player freedom?
7. Where do you personally feel the tension between "how things used to be" and "how things are now"?
8. How well do you understand the pressures your athletes navigate—social media, comparison culture, overstimulation, parental involvement?
9. Have you ever played for or worked with a coach who was clearly trying to be someone else? How did you feel around them?
10. Have you tried to explain to your team why you are the way you are as well as trying to understand them? Tell them what the norms of your generation were and how they formed your coaching mentality.

CONCLUSION

OCKER ROOMS HAVE always been more than
just places to prepare for a game—they're where lessons
about life, leadership, and character take shape. The same
environment that once shaped me as a player has continued to
shape me as a coach, and now, hopefully, through this book, it
has reached you as well.

The journey we've explored together has little time for chasing
perfection or even collecting wins; it's a journey of connection.
Great teams are defined by the depth of their relationships and
the strength of their shared purpose. When players learn to care
more about each other than themselves, they discover genuine
teamwork—and a culture that changes everything.

Every coach has the power to create that kind of environment. It happens in the small, daily moments: the way you
listen, the example you set, the consistency you model when no
one's watching. Choose to lead with humility when ego feels
easier. Stay patient when progress feels slow. Keep caring when
circumstances make it hard.

You'll find you've built far more than a successful program.
You'll build a legacy of people who carry the lessons of your

leadership into every area of their lives. A victory that lasts far beyond the final buzzer, that makes coaching one of the most meaningful callings in the world.

Team culture is a marathon, not a sprint. I often use the analogy of a boulder in the mountains. You can't split a massive rock with one swing of a hammer—but a steady stream of water can split it clean down the middle over time. A persistent habit will always be more powerful than one dramatic moment.

So, friends, this book isn't a cure-all. If you only think about these ideas today, the impact will fall short. The lessons in these pages should be applied with consistency throughout your season. If you commit to the process, your team will finish as a strong family. You'll compete in games you never believed you could. Coach, this is just the beginning of your dream season. I'm rooting for you.

TEAM CULTURE DEVELOPMENT PLAN

OVERVIEW & PURPOSE

Lead 101 is your go-to team culture development plan to launch your season with purpose. Once your rosters are finalized, begin with *Day 1* and follow the plan for *just 8 days*. By the end of it, every team member will clearly understand the expectations, roles, and values that define your group.

Starting the season united and aligned will build a strong foundation—that helps you grow and stay grounded through the inevitable challenges ahead. Set the tone now, so you're ready for what's next.

PLAN OVERVIEW

Day 1:	Team Rules & Procedures
Day 2:	Goal Setting
Day 3:	Team Leader Designation
Day 4:	Communication During Competition
Day 5:	Communication Outside of Competition
Day 6:	Game Simulation
Day 7:	Wins
Day 8:	Losses

BEST PRACTICE

Establish these attitudes prior to starting.

Be *humble* (acknowledging you have room for growth) and *curious* (having a desire to learn more). These two qualities are extremely important for development.

DAY 1: TEAM RULES & PROCEDURES

SAY

"Take a look around. This is your family for the foreseeable future. Just like any family, we will have many ups and downs. What will set this group apart from the teams on our schedule is that we will handle both the good and the bad with class and dignity. Before we can even get to those wins and losses, we have to establish rules and procedures. These aren't recommendations but expectations. The rules aren't for the coaches to have authority; they're for our team to have order. We can't get to the top of the mountain unless we start from a place of togetherness. And the only way to stay together is to all be on the same page when it comes to the expectations we have when you wear this uniform. No one is above the law. The faster you understand that these rules are for your benefit rather than to rule over you, the faster we'll find success."

TASK

On the next page write down your expectations for these three categories: in the community, in school, on this team. It's crucial that you address all three, based on the following guidelines.

COMMUNITY RULES

Establish the fact that each player represents your team wherever they go. Whether it's toilet-papering a house or causing problems at the local pool, their behavior will affect your team.

SCHOOL RULES

School rules are extremely important. The fastest way to lose a player is by bad grades or bad behavior. You need to address classroom expectations, work completion expectations, and in-school behavior expectations.

TEAM RULES

Your team rules depend on your personality. Some coaches keep it lighter than others. Regardless of your leanings, all players should be held to a high standard. Talk about communication, attitude, timeliness, and sick days.

COMMUNITY RULES

SCHOOL RULES

TEAM RULES

DAY 2: GOAL SETTING

SAY

"Vision and accountability are two of the most crucial components of leadership and development. Goal setting includes both. The selection of a goal includes vision, which is the ability to see what you'd like to be in the future. After setting the goal you need to be held accountable as you chase the goal. Some days will be better than others, but every day requires feedback of some sort."

TASK

"Today, we're all going to write out three individual goals and three team goals. When everyone has finished, we are going to share what we wrote. The coaches will compile a list, then, as a team, we'll settle on five team goals for the season. These goals can be team culture-based (positive attitude every day), stat-based (free throw percentage), or work ethic-based (lift three days per week)."

INDIVIDUAL GOAL 1

INDIVIDUAL GOAL 2

INDIVIDUAL GOAL 3

TEAM GOAL 1

TEAM GOAL 2

TEAM GOAL 3

DAY 3: TEAM LEADER DESIGNATION

Coaches, spell out for your team what your team leadership duties are. Clearly state what the responsibilities of a *captain* are for your program.

Next, decide what process you will use for this decision. The following are ways in which programs can identify their leadership:

- Players vote
- Coaches decide without input
- Seniors take turns at leading each week or each game

Decide what works for you.

SAY

"Our goal for today is to designate who our team leaders (or captains) will be for this season. An important concept to understand before we do this is that anyone can be a leader, with or without a title. The title *captain* only goes so far. The captains might represent the team before a game, but any one of you can be a strong leader. If having the title *captain* makes you a leader, then you're not a very good leader, if one at all."

TASK

Ask your team to list out what makes a good leader. Everyone should contribute at least one idea. Write what they say on the whiteboard. You now have a list of expectations to give to your leadership team.

End day 3 by telling your team who the leaders are and prepare to have a follow-up meeting with those players to discuss expectations.

DAY 4: COMMUNICATION DURING COMPETITION

ACTIVITY

Have your players put themselves in order from youngest to oldest without speaking.

After they're finished, go down the line and see how they did. Then bring them back to their seats.

SAY

"This activity was a demonstration of how much harder a simple task is without communication. Communicating is one of the most taken-for-granted aspects in sports. We think we can get away without it, but we don't realize how much harder it makes the game to play when we're silent. Just like the activity you just did in silence, we can make an easy task difficult if we remove our voices. One of the noticeable differences between average or bad teams and good teams is simply the effort to communicate. (Give examples of the kind of communication that is expected in your sport.) Communicating is a choice. It's not a skill. Every one of you has the ability to communicate."

TASK

List out the things your team is expected to communicate during a game or competition.

DAY 5: COMMUNICATION OUTSIDE OF COMPETITION

SAY

"Just as we have expectations for your communication during competitions, we also have expectations for how you communicate outside of competitions. We need to do the following for the benefit of our team.

- Text or call your coach when you're going to miss a practice. If you're too sick, have your parents contact the coach. But it should be you as far as possible.
- Discuss transportation needs *before* a game day. You should not go up to a coach the hour before heading to a game to tell them that you need to ride home with your parents. This should be done in a timely manner.
- If you need to stay after school to finish work, we can accommodate that, but we need to know in advance.
- If you have any injury, you need to let us know. Don't hide it from us. Not disclosing injuries will only hurt you more.
- If you're upset about playing time, come have that conversation with your coach. Not your buddies. Not your teachers. You need to own your issues and come talk about it. I will *not* respond to parents asking about playing time until you've asked me first. This is for no other reason than to teach you responsibilities and how to have hard conversations. He said/she said will get us nowhere good.
- Don't talk poorly about teammates. Don't complain to mom and dad that Bobby is playing more than you. Don't go down the hallways telling kids that Johnnie screwed

up a play. Keep it in the locker room. Dissension can only hurt this team.

- We are going to watch our language. Represent yourself and this team well. Not just here, but in the community too. No one is impressed with your ability to cuss."

DAY 6: GAME SIMULATION

Something I learned from a great coach early in my career was that every team should walk through every aspect of a game before the first game. The reason? We don't want any surprises or confusion on game day. The first game is not a "warm-up." It counts.

TASK

With your team, walk through every aspect of a game. It may feel silly, but it's extremely helpful.

1. Getting ready: Give them ten minutes to get into their uniforms.
2. Pregame check-in: Have them sit exactly where they'll sit for the pregame discussion and prep.
3. Warm-ups: Put time on the clock and have them go through the exact warm-up routine.
4. Anthem and lineups: Yes, we're even doing this. Play the anthem. Do a dry run of the lineup introductions if your sport does this in games.
5. Last huddle: Give specifics as to what your captains want the last huddle to look like.
6. Halftime (if your sport has one): Have your team run to the locker room. Tell them what you expect halftimes to look like. Have them walk through the halftime warm-up.
7. End of game: Finish with what post-game expectations are. Keep uniforms on. Sit together. No phones.

(Mention that on the next two days you'll discuss what wins and losses need to look like.)

Your team is now ready for that important first game.

DAY 7: WINS

ASK

Ask your team what the biggest or most fun win of their athletic career has been so far. What made it so special?

SAY

"If sports are supposed to be fun, and winning is fun, then one of the best things you can do for your experience is to win. It's ok to say that. None of us are playing to lose. So often we're afraid to say winning is important, because it might just place expectations on us to win. There is truth in the fact that you can't win every game. And yes, there are more important things. But let's get one thing clear: We want to win. We won't cheat or cut corners. But we will do everything we can to win on and off the court this season."

TASK

Discuss what it takes to win on the court.

Discuss what it takes to win off the court.

The most important part: you can't settle for just one win and celebrate it. Nick Saban had a concept that he called "relief syndrome." Relief syndrome is when, after a team wins, the players typically experience relief and rest on their laurels. Saban's biggest goal at the University of Alabama was to keep his team hungry. There's no time to rest until the season is over. Your hunger for one win has to turn into a hunger to go 1–0 every day. Stay hungry.

DAY 8: LOSSES

SAY

"One of the hardest things about being in sports is that you know when you've lost. In other jobs or activities, you can talk yourself into a win if you want to. You can sugarcoat the results. In sports, you can't mislead someone. When the game is over, there's a winner and a loser. You can't blur the black-and-white lines to make it gray.

"The first thing we have to do is *accept our part* in it. The loss doesn't define our value. No number of losses can make us worse people. Your value as a person is not contingent upon your team's record. With that said, you still have to own your shortcomings. Coaches must do the same. We will never move forward and learn from losses until we own up to our part in it. When you watch the game back, don't hide from the mistakes. Confess them and learn from them. As a coach, I will also own mine. When a strategy doesn't work, when a timeout was called poorly, when a play wasn't installed properly, I will own those things. We cannot move forward without *humility*.

"The second thing we need to do is *adjust*. If there's something you're doing individually, or we're doing as a team, that isn't working, we have to adjust. We have to be flexible, open, and smart. Throughout this season, the following things might happen: A player gets assigned a different position. We change the lineups. We alter our scheme. We add new plays. If you're not open to change, you may get left behind. If, as a coach, I'm not open to change, we will suffer. We have to acknowledge when the things we're doing aren't working. And sometimes the most powerful thing we can do is sacrifice our pride for the team.

"The third and final thing we need to do is *never quit or hang our head*. There might be a time when our loss is a really bad one. We may hit a painful losing streak. I want you to think of the season like running a marathon. There will be times when it's hard to keep pushing. You might consider quitting. The ultimate goal, whether it's going good or bad, is to cross the finish line. It does not matter too much where marathon runners place when the race is over. They're just glad they accomplished a hard task. There is pride in the feat. They trained. They endured. They finished. You *have to* finish the race this season. No matter how good or bad our record is, you need to finish strong. You will never regret not quitting. But if you quit, I guarantee you will regret it for the rest of your life. There are no do-overs. There are no second chances. No matter what, keep running until you cross that finish line."

TASK
Hand out a contract for each player to fill out.

CONTRACT

I, (print name) _______________________________,
understand that this season will be hard. I know that there will
be good times and bad times. I am prepared for the race ahead
of me. I am ready to give my all for this team.

____

Sign on the line

WRITE YOUR THREE GOALS FOR THIS SEASON

GOAL 1

GOAL 2

GOAL 3

ACKNOWLEDGMENTS

No book is ever written alone, and this one is no exception.

Thank you to my wife, Natalie, for making this possible. There are no words that accurately express your value to this project. The ways you've sacrificed so that I can chase my dreams is an act of complete, unrelenting love. You were my biggest cheerleader from the bleachers and now from home. I hope that whatever your dreams are, I can support you just as well. It's your turn next.

My sons, Griffin and Nolan, you motivate me every day. You shared your daddy's time willingly as I pursued this project. I hope you always have the courage to go after your goals, no matter what the odds of success are. Life is so short—live it to the best of your ability.

The Price family. It's in our blood to compete. We don't know what content means. Which is a double-edged sword, I must confess. But thank you for never letting me settle. Thank you, Mom, for your example of undeniable faithfulness. Thank you, Dad, for being an ardent supporter of my work.

The Nelsen family. You treat me like one of your own. You love me. You accept me for who I am. Thank you for being the perfect emotional support system. I couldn't make it through something like this without you.

Thank you to everyone else who played a role, whether it was moral support or help with the book: Jay Benish, Andrew Breen, Todd Blakeman, Caleb Cox, Alex Demzcak, Vondel Edgar, Nate Eischeid, Jon Fischer, Gus Foster, Mike Garber, Eli Gerdes, Dean Gosse, Capel Henshaw, Josh Hepler, Tom Johnson, John Karabas, Brandon Lawson, Mallory Liebl, Jay Lipe, Josh O'Connor, Jim O'Leary, Evan Penniman, Brett Pickarts, Keelin Rasch, John Standard, Johnnie Standard, Luke St. Lifer, Dakota Street, Jesse Tinch, Hudson Torrez, Austin Welz, and Jon Wiezorek.

If I left your name out, write it here: ___________________.

With gratitude,
Hunter Price

ENDNOTES

1 "Issue 76 – Don't Mistake Activity for Achievement," Wooden's Wisdom, accessed February 3, 2026, https://woodenswisdom. com/leadershipIssue.php?issue_id=76.

2 Mike Krzyzewski, *Leading with the Heart: Coach K's Successful Strategies for Basketball, Business, and Life* (Warner Business Books, 2001).

3 Jon Gordon, *The Energy Bus: 10 Rules to Fuel Your Life, Work, and Team with Positive Energy* (Wiley, 2007).

4 Jon Gordon, "Chapter 18: No Energy Vampires on the Bus," O'Reilly, accessed February 20, 2026, https://www. oreilly.com/library/view/the-energy-bus/9780470100288/ gord_9780470100288_oeb_c18_r1.html.

5 Jake Rogal, dir., "Episode 3," *Court of Gold*, Netflix, Higher Ground Productions, Olympic Channel Services & Words + Pictures, 2025.

6 Rogal, "Episode 3," *Court of Gold*.